701046

S0-CBR-080

THE WITNESS

Message, Method, Motivation

BY

URIE A. BENDER

9528

HERALD PRESS, SCOTTDALE, PENNSYLVANIA

9728

THE WITNESS

Scripture quotations indicated by "Phillips" are from *The New Testament in Modern English,* © J. B. Phillips, 1958. Used by permission of The Macmillan Company and Geoffrey Bles, Ltd.

To Dorothy, my wife,
for her unswerving support
and constant encouragement
in this way of life

CONTENTS

The grace of God has now become known—

For the grace of God, which can save every man, has now become known.

At the beginning God expressed himself. That personal expression, that word, was with God and was God, and he existed with God from the beginning. All creation took place through him, and none took place without him. In him appeared life and this life was the light of mankind. The light still shines in the darkness, and the darkness has never put it out.

A man called John was sent by God as a witness to the light, so that any man who heard his testimony might believe in the light. This man was not himself the light: he was sent simply as a personal witness to that light.

That was the true light which shines upon every man as he comes into the world. He came into the world—the world he had created—and the world failed to recognize him. He came into his own creation, and his own people would not accept him. Yet wherever men did accept him he gave them the power to become sons of God. These were the men who truly believed in him, and their birth depended not on the course of nature nor on any impulse or plan of man, but on God.

So the word of God became a human being and lived among us. We saw his splendor (the splendor as of a father's only son), full of grace and truth. And it was about him that John stood up and testified, exclaiming: "Here is the one I was speaking about when I said that although he would come after me he

7

*would always be in front of me; for he existed before I was born!"
Indeed, every one of us has shared in his riches—there is a grace
in our lives because of his grace. For while the Law was given by
Moses, love and truth came through Jesus Christ. It is true that
no one has ever seen God at any time. Yet the divine and only
Son, who lives in the closest intimacy with the Father, has made
him known. (Titus 2:11; John 1:1-18, Phillips)*

1

INTRODUCTION

Some years ago I was sitting in a university classroom listening to a lecture on philosophy. In the course of development, it grew into an attack on the Christian faith. At the close of the period, a fellow student asked for my opinion on the lecture.

Crudely perhaps, but honestly, I said, "He's all wet."

"Why?" she asked, in obvious disagreement.

In the two or three minutes it took to walk to her bus stop outside the administration building, I told LeAnn about my own personal experience of faith in Christ and my appreciation for the Bible which I believed to be God's Word.

The next day LeAnn questioned me further about my spiritual experience. And the day following she asked if we might spend several hours working together on our assignments. I agreed, but discovered quickly that this was a cover-up for her real desire to know more. This questioning attitude continued until the end of the course.

Each week came the question. "May we study together on Thursday afternoon?" And each Thursday afternoon, the study of philosophy claimed only a small portion of the time. Questions on the Christian life filled the remainder.

I found myself sharing deeply and with a strange joy. Suddenly I awoke to the fact that I had been witnessing and that it had been an enjoyable experience. A normal contact had opened itself to reveal an opportunity to share in a natural way—unforced, without pressure of any kind.

Without warning, my previous conceptions of all that witnessing involved began to crumble. Old patterns of Christian service, until now unquestioned, seemed stilted and forced instead of spontaneous and free. Something to shrink from instead of to enjoy. I was forced to revise my thinking, my practice, even my sermon outlines. From this simple experience came a revelation which brought a revolution to my life.

Since then, I have shared with others this small insight, this revolution which changed, for me, the definition of "witnessing." I have spoken of witnessing as a normal part of Christian living— an integral part of life rather than an exercise. I have tried to outline the simple Scriptural pattern which can make of this experience a joy. Occasionally, I have recounted my own adventures in witnessing.

Each time this has been my privilege, I have been deeply impressed with the evident need for a clear definition of witnessing. Again and again, following discussions, during counseling periods, in letters, troubled disciples of Christ have confessed their inability to fit into certain stereotyped methods. Though dedicated Christians, many of them echoed a stricken cry: *I can't witness. I've tried. Often. At different places. It doesn't work.*

For such these pages are written.

Some words wear well with little change in force or meaning. Others lose their intended impact during long use or through abuse. These may drop by the way. Or they may continue to be used even after they have been devalued or distorted by unwise applications. As a result, their use leads to half-truths and misunderstandings. Such a word is witness.

Witness is a good word. Correctly used, it is filled with meaning. It carries a Scriptural idea. It describes a way of life. But faulty definitions, verbal and practical, have twisted it into a dagger that can and does pierce the Christian's conscience; too often, unfortunately, at the wrong place.

In some circles, to hear the word is to wince. A discussion of the idea trips a trigger of guilt feelings and self-judgment. The promotion of witnessing, without a careful Scriptural definition, may cause one to share the condemnation of those who have helped to produce the frustration so many Christians experience.

I have never forgotten my own relief in discovering the larger dimension of witnessing—that it is not limited to a single method, stilted and forced. For me, this was a great discovery. And no less important was the truth that this new freedom made of sharing the Gospel a joyful adventure.

The problem then can be summarized in this way: Large numbers of Christians do not feel free to share their faith.

The issue behind the problem is *why not*. A few may not recognize this as an obligation. Some, through lack of commitment or because of misunderstanding, refuse. Others, many others, want to witness, try to follow some highly promoted procedure but finally give up in despair, concluding that for them witness is impossible.

Such simply assume that only "professionals" can witness. This poses a serious problem. So much emphasis has been placed on aptitudes, techniques, and systems that the ordinary person becomes witness-shy without thinking through the meaning of his withdrawal. The right word at the right time, the right verse for the right need, the right moment for the right question— together, these serve to intimidate.

Even the dedicated Christian sometimes confesses he doesn't know what to say. In fact, he is fearful he will say the wrong thing, or perhaps say the right thing in the wrong way. However, not knowing what to say is less of a problem, if every man were completely honest, than the uncertainty whether what he has to say is completely acceptable against the "norms" superficially set up. Thus the deadening curse of a Christian-worker category, as opposed to a member-of-the-body-of-Christ concept, kills the perception of need and the sense of obligation on the part of each

Christian. This binds the church of God.

However, this situation reflects but half of the problem. Leaving the task of witnessing to the pseudo-professional means that the recipient frequently faces a high-pressure approach that may be unthinking, discourteous, and even crude. He tends to form opinions regarding Christianity on the basis of this approach and, in his reaction against this pattern of witness, may then also effectively close himself off from the influences of the more genteel testimony. And thus turn his back on Christ.

In addition to questions of definition, the reasons for frustration, and the concept of natural rather than forced contacts, the thinking Christian feels a vague uneasiness in other areas as well. The matter of friendship with non-Christians; the quality of his own acceptance of others; the personhood of non-Christians; the need for involvement; the example of Christ's life and service; the values of the indirect approach—all of these and other questions crowd into his mind for attention and judgment.

What is it we have to say? How do we communicate? Why? With whom do we share? What helps can we find to lead us into a life of witnessing which will bring glory to Christ?

However, before these questions are answered, some attention should be given to the negative factors already hinted at. What keeps us from being a witness as well as from the specific experience of witnessing? Why do many Christians evade their acknowledged responsibility? Can we identify the problem and its source in our own experience? How has insistence on method throttled discipleship? In what ways have certain methods distorted Christian service?

Our world has become a neighborhood. New developments in communication have forced the Christian Church, more than ever before, to the kind of mission it should be engaged in, wherever in the world it is found. That is, basically, a person-to-person witness.

This is not to deny a world concern that reaches beyond our neat backyard fences. Nor is it to evade our Christian responsibility in the political and economic realms of the countries in which we live. But it is to emphasize that mission is carried on within one fundamental context, between individuals. Mission, the mission of Christ, however it may be stated, has no other essential dimension. Unless this personal dimension is recognized, the functional resources of Christ's body will lie latent, on the one hand. And on the other hand, the masses in need will never appear as single human beings with whom the Christian is called to relate. Failing either perspective, the objective compassion of Christ, the Head of the body, will be thwarted.

Underlying the life and action of the Christian Church, including every member of the body, is the premise that God loves men and women. His love comes to us and continues to change us into His likeness. Embedded in this continuing work of grace lies the concern of God for every one of His creatures. We, the recipients of His love, become also the channels through which flows the compassion of our Father. All we are and have become in Christ is designed to further the reconciling reach of divine grace into situations of human need.

If this is God's work, and we are His co-workers, dare we conclude that a witness of His love and power is optional—or too difficult—or impossible? Hardly. Better to join hands in exploration of the proposition that this witness is an enjoyable part of the normal Christian experience. And that it fits naturally into our everyday living. Perhaps we can learn together.

There is a right witness and a wrong witness—

If you are then "risen" with Christ, reach out for the highest gifts of Heaven, where your master reigns in power. Give your heart to the heavenly things, not to the passing things of earth. For, as far as this world is concerned, you are already dead, and your true life is a hidden one in Christ. One day, Christ, the secret center of our lives, will show himself openly, and you will all share in that magnificent dénouement.

In so far, then, as you have to live upon this earth, consider yourselves dead to worldly contacts: have nothing to do with sexual immorality, dirty-mindedness, uncontrolled passion, evil desire, and the lust for other people's goods, which last, remember, is as serious a sin as idolatry. It is because of these very things that the holy anger of God falls upon those who refuse to obey him. And never forget that you had your part in those dreadful things when you lived that old life.

But now, put all these things behind you. No more evil temper or furious rage: no more evil thoughts or words about others, no more evil thoughts or words about God, and no more filthy conversation. Don't tell one another lies any more, for you have finished with the old man and all he did and have begun life as the new man, who is out to learn what he ought to be, according to the plan of God. In this new man of God's design there is no distinction between Greek and Hebrew, Jew or Gentile, foreigner or savage, slave or free man. Christ is all that matters, for Christ lives in them all.

15

As, therefore, God's picked representatives of the new humanity, purified and beloved of God himself, be merciful in action, kindly in heart, humble in mind. Accept life, and be most patient and tolerant with one another, always ready to forgive if you have a difference with anyone. Forgive as freely as the Lord has forgiven you. And, above everything else, be truly loving, for love is the golden chain of all the virtues. Let the peace of Christ rule in your hearts, remembering that as members of the same body you are called to live in harmony, and never forget to be thankful for what God has done for you.

Let Christ's teaching live in your hearts, making you rich in the true wisdom. Teach and help one another along the right road with your psalms and hymns and Christian songs, singing God's praises with joyful hearts. And whatever work you may have to do, do everything in the name of the Lord Jesus, thanking God the Father through him. (Colossians 3:1-17, Phillips)

2

HINDRANCES TO WITNESS

Practically, the problem of *I can't witness* sprouts from varied seeds. There are definite family resemblances between the hedges which have grown up to block witness. But enough distinctive characteristics are present to suggest treatment. For our purposes here, hindrances to witness will be identified under four categories: personal, sociological, spiritual, technical.

Each area reflects problems of crucial significance. Although not all the hindrances listed here apply to every Christian, it is difficult to ignore the validity of any one as a possible answer to the problem of *I can't witness*. This is a necessary first step. Indeed, recognizing the *why* of the problem is the first long step toward *I can* and *I do*. And more importantly, to the recognition that *I am* a witness to His grace.

Personal Hindrances

Since our mission to the world hinges ultimately on the personal element, who and what we are as persons is seen to be fundamentally significant. It is clear that many factors have converged to make us the persons we have become. To some, this may seem to imply less individual responsibility.

However, a Christian turns from the temptation to succumb to a pure fatalism. He knows that he grows into personhood sometimes because of these outside influences and other times in spite of them. And he recognizes his power, through Christ, to grow into the kind of person who attracts others.

Jesus was such a person. He did not normally search out people; they came to Him. "Now the tax collectors and sinners were all drawing near to hear him" (Luke 15:1, RSV).

To be this kind of person requires that we recognize those characteristics which inhibit natural contact and thus hinder our witness. Among them may be listed:

1. *Pride*. This sin pops up in various forms. Sometimes it shows as fear of what others will think. Other times it may be a fear of failure or rebuff. Or it can emerge in the form of a moralistic approach or preachy attitude which repels. Always it carries at least a tinge of arrogance unbecoming to one who has been saved by grace.

2. *Superiority feelings*. Closely related to pride, but not necessarily synonymous, is a brazen superiority. Such persons find it easy to seak to those they consider to be inferior to themselves—culturally, economically, or personally. Unfortunately, the condescending attitude usually shows. Even where there is ease in speaking, the sense of superiority, transmitted unconsciously, becomes a barrier to wtiness. One's attitude toward others can even affect the ability and desire to listen, an indispensable part of witness.

3. *Inferiority complex*. This barrier belongs to the "pride" family as well. Without a doubt, to allow inferiority feelings to dominate one's viewpoint reflects one of the more serious defects in the life of a Christian. Few other attitudes so insult our heavenly Father. And few other hindrances so effectively block God's wish to work through us. This false humility, which really is rank immodesty, must be recognized for what it is. In actual fact, the Bible is one continuous record of God working through ordinary human beings.

4. *Bashfulness*. Some persons feel socially inadequate, usually

in the face of new situations or new people. Meeting strangers threaten the familiar comforts felt with old friends. In itself, shyness is not bad. In fact, it can show us the way to a basic principle of witness—the most natural witnessing situation is to be found with those we know best. Of course, shyness may also be an extreme form of self-consciousness which replaces God-consciousness or other-consciousness and thus hinders witness.

5. *Inability to verbalize.* Probably, for a small percentage of people, this is an honest difficulty. To put thoughts into words, to express ideas clearly, to articulate with precision, becomes a problem in any circumstance. However, most individuals are capable of expression in those areas of life where they have considerable familiarity or about which they feel deeply. It seems as if enthusiasm for a given subject usually overcomes the natural reserve which may be a part of personality. One can only conclude that this hindrance, in most cases, reflects an unfortunate spiritual poverty.

6. *Laziness.* Witnessing demands time and effort. Sometimes it calls for sacrifice and inconvenience. Invariably it requires conscious concern. The lazy Christian will find dozens of ways to evade responsibility. It takes time and effort to win the right to speak.

7. *Unfriendliness.* No more obvious hindrance could be listed. Yet no other hindrance has so sabotaged the work of Christ's body. The context of witnessing has always been friendship. No mass of religious clichés can break through an unfriendly atmosphere. Unfriendliness denies the very life of Christ in an individual and constitutes a contradiction of word or even superficial action. It can only result in a negative witness.

8. *Silent messengers.* Apart from the words spoken or the deeds done, certain silent messengers either support one's witness for Christ, or they undercut it. Such things as tone of voice, facial expressions, habits or mannerisms can completely overshadow words and communicate something far different from the message intended.

9. *Insensitive language.* The Christian witness never shrinks

from speaking as the Holy Spirit guides his lips. But without such clear directive he will be sensitive to the associations called forth by the use of certain words. Without interpretation, and one might add, without love, the use of words like *damnation* or *judgment* or *hell* at the wrong time can close the door of a heart forever. Even terms like *blood of the Lamb* and *born again* can throw up barriers to further witness. More will be said later regarding clichés and private language.

10. *Social crudity.* Too often zealous Christians approach individuals as trophies to be won rather than as persons to be befriended. Any cultured person observes certain standards of behavior when invited into another's home. The same should be true when, momentarily, others open their hearts and lives to us. We may bring them the warmth of our personalities, but we would not criticize the decor or, on the first visit, rearrange the furniture.

Sociological Hindrances

Persons make up society, the social community. This social community, of which the Christian is a part, forms the framework in which the Christian's influence exerts itself. He cannot function effectively as a Christian witness to the persons that form a society without being or becoming personally involved in that society. And, it must be emphasized, he cannot witness generally to society as a mass—but rather to persons who are a part of the whole.

Relationship to people is a "must" wherever witnessing is to be carried on. These relationships exist in a number of areas: home, neighborhood, school, job, club, professional organization, to name only a few. Each area provides a circle of acquaintances from which friendships may develop. It is within these segments of society, personally familiar to us, where the witness function is normally integrated within the relationship.

When anything intervenes to block our natural relationships to other persons within any social group of which we are a part, the witness function is also blocked. Then we are tempted to turn to less natural contacts and contrived approaches to do the job all of us agree needs to be done. At least three elements are involved here: a narrow view of society, withdrawal from society, failure to relate intelligently.

1. *Provincialism.* Any cultural group must fight constantly against the normal tendency to lapse into provincialism if it is to develop and retain awareness of the larger community. This is particularly true of denominations or sects whose heritage has become so ingrained in life and thought that it assumes the shape of a definable culture. It is not less true of the whole Christian Church. The spiritual heritage of faith in Christ, passed on to succeeding generations, so molds the Christian community that one can speak of a religious culture—a pattern of belief and behavior which comprises a way of life.

Obviously, this strength is useful in providing security, direction, and continuity. However, the very nature of a closed culture gives rise to a narrow provincialism that often ignores all that lies outside the gate, so to speak. When this condition persists, members of this culture tend to forget there are other cultures. Vision seldom rises beyond familiar boundaries. Fear of the unfamiliar quickly chills any possible interest in the community outside. This always results in practical isolation, as effective as if social taboos were consciously designed or an accident of fate or a quirk of geography had marooned the culture on an island.

2. *Isolation.* The isolation of the Christian Church, and specifically of individual Christians from needy hearts, constitutes a withdrawal from mission. Disengagement in terms of contact has led to uninvolvement in terms of life. This, in turn, has resulted in irrelevance in terms of message. Put more bluntly, no contact means no relationship. Lack of relationship means that what we say may have little relevance to need. If the message is irrelevant, the essential work of Christ's body, the church, is negated and of no effect. Against the background of God's plan for the universe, no other situation could be more pathetic.

The Christian cannot expect to witness effectively at arm's length. Ezekiel was asked to sit for seven days where the people

sat. "Then I came to them of the captivity of Telabib, that dwelt
by the river of Chebar, and I sat where they sat, and remained
there astonished among them seven days" (Ezekiel 3:15). We
must know something about where people sit, where life is raw
and demanding. We must involve ourselves to the point of understanding their need. We must touch the world and not be too
busy to be touched ourselves.

Unless our isolation is broken down, whether geographical,
linguistic, social, or intellectual, the church cannot do its work.
It has literally lost contact with the very people whom it has been
commissioned to reach. Souls are not being saved. So we console
ourselves by remembering the prediction of closed ears and stony
hearts in the last days. Or we become discouraged and, with a
mental shrug, conclude secretly that the Gospel is no longer
fully operative in this day. This is not the case! We have simply
not maintained contact with those whom God is seeking to bring
into His family.

Recently a Christian lady was heard to boast of the fact that
she had not one non-Christian friend. Such a testimony reflects a
complete misunderstanding of discipleship. Unfortunately, she is
not alone in her exclusive unfriendliness.

Very few Christian people have non-Christian friends—
acquaintances, yes; but not friends. Those who do are sometimes
looked down upon. Those who do not are frequently active in
the church's formal program. Yet it is often the activistic group
in a congregation that is singularly unsuccessful in reaching the
lost. And it seems that the nonactivists—the friends of sinners—
are living and functioning at least in a climate where true witness
is possible.

Jesus told of a concerned shepherd. This shepherd looked for
the lost sheep—the one lost sheep. To be really concerned about
witnessing requires us to think of people as individuals rather
than in the mass. To ignore the individual in favor of the masses
condemns us to a practical isolationism.

Still another kind of isolationism is illustrated by the pro-
tective fences we have built around ourselves. These have not

always accomplished their original purposes. But they have succeeded admirably in protecting Christians from redemptive contacts. Christ calls us to leave the tiny circles of our separated
comfort and get next to the dirt and corruption, the worldliness,
the hostilities, the pursuit of power; in short, the world of today.
Social ills, spiritual disorientations, economic dislocations
demand our personal attention. If the Gospel is powerful, as we
claim it to be, then our task is to find ways to unleash that power
in relevant application to the situations in which man finds
himself.

This does not mean a breaking down of the clear line
between a life of sin and a life of discipleship. But it does mean
that the isolation of the Christian—the barriers to contact—must
be broken down so that God's grace can flow through to the need.

The concern for separation between the Christian and the
world is understandable and Scriptural. But is there not a difference between "love of the world" and "loving our neighbor"? Is
there not a place for redemptive friendships with those who have
never known the strength of God's love or meaning in life or
freedom from guilt? Cannot separation from the world be maintained without the isolation that makes separation an end in
itself?

Paul speaks to this point. I Corinthians 5:9-11. He had been
misunderstood earlier. Apparently people took his concern for
separation to mean they should not associate with immoral men.
He explains that he was referring to this kind of person in the
church. And he reminds his readers that to stop associating with
sinners they would have to leave the world. Yet the same misunderstanding exists today. Various plans are set up to isolate the
Christian from the unbeliever. Nothing is more dishonoring to
God than this denial of His redemptive purpose.

Involvement implies continuity. Of course, a witness can be,
should be, and often is, given in a transient context. But the witness which really speaks with impact is usually that witness continued during a series of contacts which have grown in a more or
less natural way. For some strange reason, Christian workers have

been encouraged in patterns of witnessing to people with whom they do not naturaly associate. This often forces a transient witness. It would seem that the people we work with or spend time with, regular associates, are the ones for whom we should have the greatest concern, and also the greatest opportunity for witness. This appears to be a more natural method than to make a mechanical selection of groups based on economic status, geography, education, business interest, or any other category.

This points to a fundamental principle in witnessing. We witness best where we move within a context of friendliness, often friendship. Friends, of course, are not acquired automatically. We must work at developing friendships. And until we have friends among non-Christians we are not in a very good position to witness.

When rapport develops, then witnessing becomes much more than a junior sermon, a series of proof texts, or a pious moralism. It becomes a mutual sharing, a dialogue. With interaction and response, communication takes place, which, after all, is our objective. But communication requires an atmosphere of confidence. Confidence is built into relationship.

To retreat into an insulated stockade may seem desirable. But to turn from this isolation and advance into involvement costs a great deal. It forces limitation of interests; it creates misunderstandings; it insists on denial and sacrifice; it often calls for suffering; it requires time—in many cases great amounts of time; it literally demands our life. This is what involvement in the needs of men cost Christ and it will cost us no less. From this we tend to shrink.

3. *Communication barriers.* Language forms an integral part of any culture. It serves as a medium of control, idea interaction, and thought transference. It conveys the sum total of culture from one generation to another. Whether primitive or highly developed, it is a part of the social scene in every community.

Although various members of a cultural community possess different degrees of ability to understand language, one can generalize and say that within a given linguistic community, everyone understands the language. However, whenever any one individual moves from his own culture to another culture, he will find a new world. Very likely his attempts at communication, at least in precise forms, will be quite unsuccessful. If he lives in the new culture for a while, he will begin to relate his own cultural symbols of expression to those of the new culture. If he puts forth real effort, he may even become acquainted with many details of the new culture which should result in increased understanding and insights. Eventually, his knowledge of both cultures, the old and the new, enables him to become a bridge of understanding between these cultures.

To simplify discussion, let us call the old Culture A and the new Culture B. Let us assume that Culture A has developed to the point where it could make a technical and intellectual contribution to less-developed Culture B. This could be a description of how to make a wheel or it could be the scientific formula for a drug to cure cancer. Let us assume further that Culture A wishes to share these pieces of information, for whatever selfish or humanitarian reasons it may have. At this point, then, there is only one way to make this contribution: through the one person who, native to Culture A, has acquired an understanding of Culture B. Thus he becomes the sole channel by which technical and intellectual benefits can be transferred.

Too many Christians forget or ignore the obvious lesson here. Or they have not taken the time to learn it. To illustrate further, let Culture A represent the Christian community and Culture B, the non-Christian world.

As presently carried on, evangelism or witnessing leaves much to be desired. We, in Culture A, pitch a tent on the edge of Culture B and expect the members of that culture to be curious enough at least to peek inside. Or we set up a loudspeaker to blare forth in our language, the benefits we presume to possess. Or we make hurried trips on a Sunday afternoon into Culture B to buttonhole people or to hand out pieces of paper while the objects of our frantic and scattered efforts read or listen to our strange gibberish with, at best, a tolerant air. Or we move in an army of people-counters so that we can fill our files and report statistics. Or we hire an architect to plan an asset to the community. Who can deny that Christian workers sometimes act like a fisherman dangling a hook on main street and calling to fish in the river a mile away? "Come, my dears, won't you bite my little hook?"

Occasionally, as statistics show, there is communication. But too often this seems to be almost by accident rather than design.

On the one hand, one must concede that this picture is over-drawn to accent what should be obvious. On the other hand, however, the caricature may be pathetically close to reality. Our provincial attitudes and our practical isolation have built barriers to communication. Instead of moving into Culture B as permanent residents, by design we have remained transients with few real points of contact. Of course, this is a problem in non-religious areas as well. But we cannot ignore the application to the Christian Church in light of the essential nature of witness in its life.

The world is full of what someone has called "linguistic pluralism." All of us recognize a variety of languages and dialects in the world—thousands of them. But not many are aware of the existence, within a single language, of private languages. This is true of English, for example.

Call a meeting of representative natives from Brooklyn, New York; Georgetown, British Guiana; Hazard, Kentucky; London, England; Lubbock, Texas; Windsor, Ontario; and Lancaster, Pennsylvania. Each one speaks English fluently. Of course, differences in speech rhythm, pronunciation, and vowel emphasis would be obvious. But in addition, words would be used, English words, quite unfamiliar to others in the group. While the majority of words spoken would communicate with fair precision, enough strange words would be injected, or familiar words with different meanings, to constitute the beginnings of a private language. Colloquialisms first, then dialect, and eventually another language.

Bring together an average teenager and an average sixty-year-old. The young person would use many words familiar to the older adult but with meanings quite foreign. Or Grandfather could recall words and terms current in his youth altogether unfamiliar to the teenager.

Listen to an electronics expert speaking to a roomful of men in the field of electronics. Note the private language. Attend a meeting of psychiatrists discussing their profession. List the words and concepts unknown to you. Ask an internist for a description, in professional language, of certain bodily processes. Then attempt to repeat his meaning. Most of us can make fair attempts at understanding because of general training or experience. But unless we have become thoroughly acquainted with the world of the electronics expert, the psychiatrist, or the internist, we will be forced to concede that parts of his language are quite private to his profession or skill. And consequently they are foreign to us.

The Christian also uses a private language based on Scriptural concepts and experience. It is a perfectly good language understood by almost every one with a more or less similar spiritual heritage. This language serves a useful purpose so long as its use is limited to Culture A—the Christian community. But when, without translation, it is projected into Culture B—non-Christian groups—the result is misunderstanding or non-understanding overlaid with a thin tolerance.

For example, look at the following approaches to the unsaved. Try to envision your own reaction to these words, had you never enjoyed a spiritual heritage: *your righteousness is as filthy rags—you are a lost sinner—you are dead in your sins—do you have the assurance of salvation? do you have the joy of sins forgiven? have you been born again? are you justified? have you taken the plunge into the crimson flow? are you living in hope of the rapture? this is the end time—you need to get under the blood—you need to come to the mercy seat—you must kneel in the shadow of the cross—I just want to tell you about the night I saw the light.*

Unfortunately, Christians appear to assume that non-Christians are specially gifted and able to understand the symbols of another culture. Or they consider it the responsibility of non-Christians to decipher the meanings of words used in our private religious language in spite of the fact that they may have little interest in it. Either view is ridiculously immature.

If Culture A has a message for Culture B, then Culture A must become acquainted with Culture B. In this way bridges of understanding can be built. Dialogue can be carried on. Communication can take place. And finally, a relevant application of spiritual truth can be made to need. Until and unless this takes place, the Christian mission ends in failure.

Most mission boards place a great deal of emphasis on a missionary's thorough acquaintance with his adopted culture. Among other things, this requires arduous and continuous study of the language. Why? Because the missionary's primary business is communication of the Gospel. And it is recognized that communication cannot take place without a knowledge of the culture to which he addresses his message. But, for some reason, the point of this lesson is missed almost completely in the context of bridging the gap between the Christian culture and the non-Christian world.

Communication is based on at least two fundamental factors: understanding and participation. Neither is possible in isolation. The Christian must move close enough to his spiritually needy friend so that the witness of life as well as the comment he may eventually make will have relevance. Because each has come to understand, in some measure, the world or culture of the other, the grace of God begins to make sense with reference to particular circumstances. Here is communication. And herein lies the mission of the church.

Spiritual Hindrances

A Christian witness has obvious spiritual implications. The essence of witness is to report a miracle of grace. The "master of ceremonies" in witness is the Holy Spirit. The concern of witnesses is the spiritually needy hearts in the world.

Since a witness to the grace of God is really a spiritual exercise, one must recognize the possibility of spiritual hindrances blocking its fulfillment. These are varied but similarly destructive to the Christian's fundamental purpose in life.

1. *Uncertainty about our own salvation.* Doubt here cuts the vital nerve of a Christian's witness. Doubt puts the Christian in the position of proclaiming a "maybe" message. At best this is no message and at worst is a negative message. Doubt destroys initiative, drains enthusiasm, and communicates only itself. Doubt devastates the best efforts to share because it shares only a shell.

The non-Christian begs for certainty, for assurance, for solid ground somewhere. To announce the fact of God's grace in a testimony laced with doubt is a teasing treachery, unworthy of the Christian Gospel.

No one unsure of salvation is a witness except to his own lack of assurance. Only he can speak who has himself confessed his own sin and utter helplessness. Who has experienced and is experiencing the lifting, healing, cleansing power of God's love. Who, in his lostness, has been found. Who, out of his searching, has discovered the Way. Who, from the deep despair of his aimlessness, has awakened to meaning. Who has been saved from himself, in Jesus' name. Every other tongue is tied, and justifiably so.

2. *Unwillingness.* Whether such a point should be included in this list is debatable. Is unwillingness to witness actually a problem to the child of God? Are there Christians unwilling to share? Can a person receive forgiveness without responding in obedience? Is not the term "unwilling disciple" a paradox?

Ideally, the disciple is always willing. However, who of God's family does not face the temptation to self-will? This can become a deadening barrier to usefulness as a member of Christ's body. Willfulness blocks the will and work of God's Spirit. Unyieldedness frustrates the ministry of sharing. Lack of discipleship denies the lordship of Christ, the very heart of the message. Only a full application of God's grace can make the witness willing and his testimony effective.

3. *Lack of boldness.* To remain a spectator in the arena of Christian service requires little courage. But to step into the battle, to engage the forces of evil, calls for greater than human resources.

There is a boldness to speak which is human and which, in itself, often becomes a hindrance. Nothing is gained and usually much is lost when boldness is simply an expression of human personality or is mistakenly assumed to be a desirable character- istic and consequently cultivated. The boldness to be coveted by Christians goes beyond the blunt and crude confrontations of zealous but ignorant would-be witnesses. Such boldness dishonors God and seldom attracts unbelievers.

However, the Scriptures teach a holy boldness which reflects, not human defect, but a spirit of quiet confidence and humble fearlessness born of the Spirit of God. Far from arrogance, it commands respect and demands a hearing. It ignores threats, overrides personal hesitations, and bypasses possible distortions of message. It speaks, not to intimidate, but simply because the message must be given.

Complete dependence upon the Holy Spirit is basic. He must control. Unfortunately, many Christians speak when silence would be far better. Many more are silent in crucial moments when a few words, born of God and spoken in love and faith, could change the direction of a life.

4. *Embarrassment.* Closely related to lack of boldness is embarrassment. To be embarrassed when discussing spiritual matters may be related to personal shyness. Or it may have its roots in spiritual need or misunderstanding. The latter two possibilities are our concern here.

A common misconception is that witnessing requires fluency of speech and correct theological terms. Neither is a valid require- ment. Most non-Christians are very ordinary people (as are most Christians), with average abilities and little evidence of real brilliance in any field. These are our neighbors and friends, the ones with whom we seek to share. Among many of these, fluency would tend to overwhelm and perhaps even set up barriers. A sincere word, haltingly spoken under the Spirit's guidance, is far more eloquent than any lengthy outburst of words. Enough has been said about private language and evangelical jargon to show that "proper" terms must be translated anyway.

Sometimes embarrassment comes because we forget who we are and whom we represent. The King of heaven sends us into the world as ministers of reconciliation, as ambassadors for Christ. This high calling, this noble station cannot tolerate embarrassment—a denial of the majesty and glory of His name we bear.

Perhaps a more serious cause for embarrassment is an inconsistent life. The life a Christian lives is always on display. Every aspect of it carries a message. To be intelligible, the message cannot have contradictory elements.

5. *Unfamiliarity with the Scriptures.* The Word of God stands central among the tools used by the Christian witness. No other available resource can replace the Bible. The impact of its message reaches hearts when every other approach has failed.

This calls for thorough acquaintance with the Word. However, lest there be misunderstanding, let it be said quickly that witnessing does not demand the scholar's mind. Nor does God ask only for a human memory bin in which to store up "verses." Scholarship and memorization are important, but in this context, not as ends in themselves. The Word of God will be studied and meditated upon for its own sake and one's own spiritual growth. Both scholarship and memorization can and likely will be by-products of this approach. And out of this treasure, made personally meaningful, will flow a sharing with others, spontaneous and relevant.

Familiarity with the Scripture grows out of a deep love for the Scriptures. A love that leads to a saturation of the soul with its message. A love that demands time spent mining its riches. A love reflected in the response of obedience to its precepts. Failing this, acquaintance with the Word of God is only mechanical and superficial. But when love of the Word is present, systems of use and techniques of witness fade into a secondary place.

What matters then if one remembers the exact sequence of steps to take with an inquiring heart? What matters then if the rules are broken by a sudden prompting of the Spirit of God? What matters then if the proper words are forgotten in the rush of personal thanksgiving for God's grace?

The Word of God hidden in the heart and dwelt upon in the quiet hours of meditation, will burst forth again and again. The freshness and relevance of the Word cannot help carrying its own message to the seeker. However, such spontaneity in remembering the Word comes only after immersion in it.

6. *Ignorance of God's purposes.* To know God brings life eternal. To understand His purposes is to find meaning for life. To yield to His will is to share in the fulfillment of His plan for the world.

But the perception of Christians sometimes is limited to the following superficial view of the church: *Christians form congregations and denominations. Appointed missionaries bring the Gospel to foreign lands. If enough dollars are given to enough missionaries in enough places, everybody can be saved. But that won't happen because it costs too much money and there aren't enough missionaries. Furthermore, who would be left to give if everyone became a missionary?*

Paul, writing to the Christians at Ephesus, describes in part God's grand design for the entire universe: "the mystery of his will . . . a plan for the fullness of time, to unite all things in him [Christ] . . . far above all rule and authority and power and dominion, and above every name that is named, not only in this age but also in that which is to come; and he has put all things under his feet and has made him the head over all things for the church, which is his body, the fulness of him who fills all in all" (Ephesians 1:9-23, RSV).

Christ has been named both the cornerstone and the keystone of history. All life has sprung from Him and all of life shall be consummated in Him. He, who is our fullness, has called us to share with Him in completing His redemptive work. His mission continues through us. We are a significant part of God's great plan for mankind to be fulfilled in Christ. This great and glorious calling is ours. Who would ask a higher meaning to life?

7. *Failure in the past.* This can become a hindrance to witness. One method is tried, then another. Attempt after attempt is made to fulfill the obligation to share. Each seems to end in failure. The pressure of commitment along with periodic urgings from the pulpit and the frustration of repeated failures combine to form a crushing discouragement which leads to a silent vow never to try again. Thus is erected a barrier almost impervious to exploration of any method of witnessing.

8. *Improper motivation.* While motivation for any action is usually hidden to some degree, many words and deeds also reflect motivation to the astute observer. One of the hindrances to witness can be wrong reasons for doing the right thing. Unless these hindrances are removed, our witness will seldom be either successful or enjoyable. Following are four motivating factors which should be questioned seriously. At another point we shall look further at the matter of primary and secondary motivations.

a. Witness by outside direction rather than by inner compulsion. To do the right thing is always commendable. Yet to witness only because one is told to witness misses the point completely. This makes a farce of that which should be sacred and meaningful. The essence of witness is not an exercise to be engaged in with regularity. It is life, all of life. There is never a moment when we do not witness—the question is only, What message are we communicating? Witness for Christ is the sum total of our influence for Christ and not a parroting of certain words at specific times. The totality of life involvement in witness requires an inner compulsion; otherwise, nothing but a joyless, mechanical exercise results.

b. Attempting to meet personal needs. Every individual has certain personality needs. Sometimes the Christian finds the process of sharing ministers to his own needs primarily. So he eagerly pursues his unsuspecting victims in a vain effort to satisfy some deep personal need or to follow some neurotic tendency under cover of holy services. This can be spiritually devastating.

c. Statistical concerns. The American culture has made
Christians number conscious. We tend to interpret progress with
relation to dollar budget, membership increase, community
census, attendance at services. This has driven individuals to
measure the quality of their witness by how many times they
have succeeded in getting a man to his knees to pray the sinner's
prayer.

Statistical concerns have their place. But they are utterly
out of place as motivation to witness. Unbelievers are not objects
to be acted upon, their sinful scalps appended to some ecclesiastical belt. They are individuals—people to be loved for themselves.
Loved in their need; loved in spite of their need. They are souls
who need friendship rather than statistics to satisfy the materialistic urges of greedy head-counters.

d. Fighting ideologies. Certain well-meaning but misguided
Christians spend their time and efforts fighting "isms." This
becomes the propelling force in their lives, coloring every activity
and utterly distorting the meaning of the Gospel. Good examples
of this are the militant rightist movements that see everything in
terms of democracy (U.S. brand) and communism. Under the
guise of a spiritual ministry, a program is carried on. Purportedly,
this constitutes a witness and the patriotic concern to free
America from the creeping tentacles of communism constitutes
the motive. Within a political context, such a motive could
stand without question. But is it worthy to stand with the Christian's primary motivations to share Christ? Christ Himself spent
much more time showing God's goodness to people than He did
fighting evil in its political or other overt forms.

9. Self-love. Loving self leads to living for self—selfish living.
North Americans need look no further to find a major block to
effective witness. The problem shows itself not only in the small
percentage of our income we share with others. Just as significant
and even more condemning is the persistent preoccupation with
material concerns. This leaves practically no time for the kind
of friendships in which witness opportunities can grow.

Paul writes of this problem to the church at Philippi (Philippians 2:19-21) and analyzes it further in the second letter to Corinthian Christians (II Corinthians 5:14, 15).

Speaking of Timothy in the first passage, he says, ". . . I have no one like him, who will be genuinely anxious for your welfare. They all look after their own interests, not those of Jesus Christ" (RSV).

In the second passage Paul writes of Christ's death, ". . . And he died for all, that those who live [become spiritually alive] might live no longer for themselves but for him who for their sake died and was raised" (RSV).

The blessing of prosperity has turned to a curse. The very advantages which should provide more freedom to develop friendships with non-Christians have become our masters. We are bound by installment contracts to the god of accumulation. And the new leisure has become a bottomless pit into which we throw large chunks of our lives without a thought of sharing these portions with those calling out of their loneliness and lostness for some love and a light to walk by.

"They all look after their own interests, not those of Jesus Christ" could be written of countless Christians this year, were Paul here to observe. The devilish selfishness of our culture has permeated the lives of Christians to an alarming degree. To rid ourselves of this barrier to witness will require honesty and courage.

10. *Disunity among Christians.* The prayer of Christ highlights this problem. "Neither pray I for these alone, but for them also which shall believe on me through their word; that they all may be one; as thou, Father, art in me, and I in thee, that they also may be one in us: *that the world may believe that thou hast sent me*" (John 17:20, 21).

Here Christ reflects the divine assignment given Him by the Father and His own concern that the assignment be carried out by His followers. Upon the union of individuals with God and the consequent unity with each other hangs the credibility of Christ's mission to the world. Tenuous thread!

The impact of this truth escapes most of us too easily. In

the place of unity we are tempted to emphasize organization. Mission boards are formed. Mission committees are elected. Missionaries are appointed. Mission budgets are established. And although we cannot ignore God's work through these means, we must decry the trend wherever it is followed in the stead of a holy unity in Christ by which men will recognize the saviorhood of Christ. If as much prayer and effort were expended in working toward unity as is spent in organized programs, we might well see a revolution in outreach. But the egotistical comfort of our divisions makes difficult the facing of adjustments required by unity.

Our evasion of the principle inherent in Christ's prayer constitutes one of the most formidable barriers to witness. Unity between Christians becomes an unanswerable argument supporting the reconciling power of God's love. Disunity nullifies the message and reduces it to a noisy annoyance—a sounding brass or a tinkling cymbal.

TECHNICAL HINDRANCES

The word "technical" may seem out of place in a discussion of witnessing. Yet so much has been said and written about technique that one dare not ignore the concept. Indeed, the crux of our concern rests at this point. Technique and definition are inextricably intertwined. Technique sprouts from definition. When definitions are incorrect or less than Scriptural, misunderstandings result. Sometimes these grow into monstrosities utterly foreign to the character of our heavenly Father.

These misunderstandings may be discussed under at least four major headings:

1. *Insistence on a single method.* At times, one is impressed with a rank spirit of competition among "soul-winners." Not only is the number of responses considered to be a reflection of success. The "success" points to the "rightness" of a method or technique or approach.

Many times when the Lord has blessed even the blundering efforts of a sincere heart, it is assumed that every subsequent contact must flow along the same lines. Other times sheer human ambition has produced some kind of response and the technique followed is quickly promoted as the right way to witness. In neither case may the individual Christian be aware that his contact has been simply the work of the human spirit or that God has blessed in spite of his efforts rather than because of his efforts. Both roads, however, can lead almost imperceptibly to a rigid insistence that no other pattern is correct.

Variations of this theme provoke a full range of twisted rationalizations that seem to ignore the teaching of Holy Scripture. And, in the process, they warp the Christian's understanding of his mission in the world. At the one extreme are those who promote the mass approach exclusively—great meetings, worldwide broadcasting or massive literature distribution programs. At the other extreme are those who are convinced that an oral testimony is seldom, if ever, necessary; that just living the Christian life constitutes witness. These usually support the contention —actual or implied—that only ordained persons and appointed missionaries are called to serve actively in the mission of the church.

Of course, each of these ideas has merit in itself. But taken out of proper context, removed from related and supporting truths, each becomes a lie. Herein lies the treachery which deceives multitudes of sincere and dedicated Christians.

2. *Stereotyped image of witnessing.* This is the child of insistence on a single method. In many Christian circles there is only one pattern of witnessing taught and practiced. And from this issues the vexing problem to which these pages are directed.

For a number of years I shared and promoted this impression. And I also suffered a great deal of the frustration which seems to follow almost inevitably. According to supporters of this view, a Christian bears a specific, personal, and immediate obligation for the spiritual welfare of every unsaved individual he meets. This calls for a careful stalking of the prey to find or provide an opening in the conversation for inquiry into his spiritual welfare. Or to the faithful witness whose training or temperament may not allow for the questionable polish of parry and thrust, sudden fear thrusts him upon his hapless quarry with an ambiguous pounce, "Brother, are you a Christian?"

This process is repeated as many times in a day or a week as there are contacts, or as a commitment may call for. In some cases each contact is a painful experience which only emphasizes the depth of dedication. In other cases, the stock question is tossed at every comer glibly, with a thoughtlessness apparently oblivious to circumstances, propriety, or the quiet urgings of the Spirit of God.

Unfortunately, such zeal frequently is not satisfied with the normal contacts of life but must contrive contacts. Appropriately, the theory of personal obligation for every sinner requires systematic coverage. This calls for door-to-door work. The housewife is called from the kitchen sink, the husband from his newspaper. To each comes the overbearing and, to many, the puzzling inquiry, "Are you saved?" When the block is covered, and reports of indifference, slammed doors, and an occasional expression of interest are turned in, the duty of evangelism in the area is assumed to be completed.

A caricature serves to highlight certain features, many times humorously. But on occasion a caricature loses its humor because it comes so close to the truth. Although never intended to be precise, it has a way of highlighting what we can see only when we see ourselves as others see us. Perhaps an application can be made here.

3. *Personality differences.* Another phase of the problem, not as easily dramatized, but certainly as significant, is the less forward nature of many Christians. One dare not forget that so-called sensitivities may be of Satan and a result of his efforts to hamper a testimony. But there still remains, in many honest and committed Christians, a distaste for the required intrusion into the intimacy of a person's life so often implied in the approach outlined above. Respect for personality and common courtesy should never submerge the clear leading of the Spirit of God. But neither are they suddenly rendered invalid by a

technique which sometimes seems to ignore certain basic Scriptural principles related to witness.

The salesman's method, applied to witnessing, may have certain advantages. But it overlooks the fact that a great many Christians will never become good salesmen because they are not temperamentally suited to use the aggressive approach so highly developed in some sales fields. The indirect approach allows for these personality differences precisely because it speaks less strongly to the point of method.

The Spirit of God can never be bound by method. Apart from the infinite variety of people serving and of people being served, there is the inexhaustible potential for unpredictable and differing situations wherever human beings are involved. Beyond this yet lies God's own infinity which, by its very nature, cannot be contained in human or finite systems.

The Spirit of God works in the individual. This results not in a rigid uniformity within the Christian society. Rather, the full flower of personality begins to bloom when a man yields himself to God. To constrict the outflowing of this life and the ways in which it contributes to the building of the church may easily do violence to the personality. Certainly, it tends to ignore the promise of the Holy Spirit for guidance to the child of God.

4. *Mechanical placement of non-Christians into categories.* Some courses in soul-winning place people into certain categories. Every conceivable kind of contact is listed with a neat packet of Scripture references tagged with the sinner's name. The serious soul-winner is expected to learn the list of categories, memorize the Scripture portions, and thus prepare himself for his forays into the world.

Along with this, highly organized approaches are outlined with every eventuality prepared for. Possible responses are predicted. Individuals are taught how to overcome fear, how to break down reserve, how to open a soul-winning conversation with ease. They learn to recognize and avoid traps which will sidetrack the conversation. They are instructed how to control the conversation with the prospect and to measure his reactions.

Demonstrations are carried out so that individuals may see this plan in action and recognize the skills they will need in a soul-winning situation. They learn to handle transition lines and key phrases. They have laboratory experiences in the classroom. They are offered elaborate plans with well-defined steps that are assumed to meet the needs of every individual they meet.

It is true that people, by nature, fall into certain categories. Many offer excuses parroted by thousands of others. Certain Scripture verses do have a pointed message for specific needs. And Scripture memorization is invaluable. But to departmentalize blocks of God's Word and to label in advance the people one is likely to meet tends to be machinelike. Often, in cases like this, the Spirit's work seems to be ignored.

The direct approach, with its variety of patterns, faces several problems. The most obvious is the complexity of some systems. Believing that a given approach being promoted is the only way to witness, they make a few feeble attempts to memorize, then throw up their hands in despair. In doing so, they turn their backs not only on a technique but many times also on their responsibility and their opportunities. Christians in this predicament could be witnesses if they had not been misled in the definition of the word.

But perhaps the essential difficulty is that no system can be tailored precisely to take into account all the fine points of varied and individual experiences. Each person meets God against the background of a rather private world, even though certain needs are universal and certain responses are basic to the human situation. When the great change takes place in a heart, no one can really devise a pattern of sharing which does not tend to throttle spontaneity. And when the sharing heart meets a need, no one can predict the ebb and flow of emotions and circumstances well enough to insist on a certain sequence in procedure.

God is never bound by any method. From Eden to the cross and from Olivet to the nuclear age, He has shown Himself, in countless ways, as a God of love and infinite concern. Certainly,

He may direct His child to a specific person with a given word of testimony. Or His will may be done through careful and systematic coverage of some rural or urban area. Without a doubt, many have been used effectively by the Spirit because they have been taught how to approach different types of individuals. And the Word of God hidden in the heart is brought to memory with telling impact in the moment of testimony.

The alert Christian recognizes the promptings of the Spirit. He is not afraid to move out in faith even though outward circumstances make his actions appear to be ridiculous. When the Spirit of God directs him to speak, he speaks. He finds no excuse to be cowardly. If bluntness is God's way of dealing with a soul, he does not shrink from being the mouthpiece.

But this is simply not the whole story. Because so often it is considered to be, countless Christians carry feelings of guilt because they seem to fall short of one pattern held up as a norm. Many live through weeks, months, years, perhaps even a lifetime, feeling the condemnation of those who insist the frontal approach is the only way to be a true witness for Jesus Christ. Regret and discouragement crowd out the joy of the Lord. Each new attempt ends in failure and leads to increasingly feeble efforts until resignation sets in.

This is the problem many would-be witnesses face. Can an ordinary Christian participate in Christ's mission to a lost world? Is there a way? Does this require appointment by a mission board or ordination by a conference? Does it demand special skills or theological training? Is a certain system necessary? Must the Christian force himself to witness?

Or is there another answer?

I think there is. I believe God expects all of His children to witness to His grace in their lives. But this witness need not be a forced exercise. Nor does it necessarily require elaborate and special preparation. The sharing will grow out of life itself and be reflected constantly through the normal contacts of everyday living. It will be an enjoyable experience, a natural part of the Christian life. It will be a daily adventure of faith and expectancy.

What does the word "witness" mean? What constitutes witnessing?

Witness (verb transitive)—to see or know by personal experience.

Witness (verb intransitive)—to bear witness: to give evidence.

Witness (noun)—a person who has seen or knows something and is therefore competent to give evidence concerning it.

Peter said, as recorded by Luke, ". . . We cannot but speak the things which we have seen and heard" (Acts 4:20).

John wrote, "That which we have seen and heard declare we unto you" (I John 1:3).

No mention is made of organization, program, or elaborate technique. Oddly enough, nothing is said about Scripture memorization or careful selection of certain sequences. Nor is there any hint of requiring a response.

Indeed, there are only two basic elements which emerge from these definitions: knowledge from personal experience and the giving of evidence based on that knowledge. That is all.

That is all!

The rest of this page properly should be left blank in order for this to make its impact on the mind. The stark simplicity of the revelation may provoke a barrage of reaction from supporters of systems. And at first it may overwhelm the Christian so long frustrated in sharing his testimony. That is, until the message grips him and transforms a hopeless drudgery into an exciting adventure. ENDING

Although witness may be an element in any one of these, witnessing is not defined precisely as:

1. Ringing doorbells in a community survey.
2. Handing out pieces of literature.
3. Asking an individual if he is born again.
4. Quoting the customary soul-winning passages.
5. Preaching a brief sermon filled with moralistic advice.
6. Asking for a response of commitment.
7. Getting a person to his knees.

I repeat. In the strictest sense of the word, from the viewpoint of both the dictionary and the Scriptures, witness is none of these. One witnesses when he gives evidence based on knowledge gained from experience. In the Christian context one witnesses when he shares his knowledge of God's grace based on his own experiences of faith in Christ.

This stands in simple contrast to frequent discussions of witness in which a central place is occupied by definition of motivation, organization of programs, and evaluation of technique.

To witness is to share. Haltingly, perhaps. Without polish, usually. Out of experience, always.

No gimmicks. Not in a forced or unnatural way. But in all of life, through word and deed, the Christian reflects the operation of the grace of God upon and within and through him.

To be brought into the family of God is to be given the blessed privilege of inviting others. To have received this love is to want to share it. To have experienced His cleansing grace and great forgiveness is to long for this release from guilt and sin for those still bound and burdened. To know His joy and power in daily living is to radiate the very presence of God.

This is witness.

The lad shared what he had—

After this, Jesus crossed the lake of Galilee (or Tiberias), and a great crowd followed him because they had seen the signs which he gave in his dealings with the sick. But Jesus went up the hillside and sat down there with his disciples. The Passover, the Jewish festival, was near. So Jesus, raising his eyes and seeing a great crowd on their way toward him, said to Philip, "Where can we buy food for these people to eat?" (He said this to test Philip, for he himself knew what he was going to do.)

"Ten dollars' worth of bread would not be enough for them," Philip replied, "even if they had only a little each."

Then Andrew, Simon Peter's brother, another disciple, put in, "There is a boy here who has five small barley loaves and a couple of fish, but what's the good of that for such a crowd?"

Then Jesus said, "Get the people to sit down."

There was plenty of grass there, and the men, some five thousand of them, sat down. Then Jesus took the loaves, gave thanks for them and distributed them to the people sitting on the grass, and he distributed the fish in the same way, giving them as much as they wanted. When they had eaten enough, Jesus said to his disciples, "Collect the pieces that are left over so that nothing is wasted."

So they did as he suggested and filled twelve baskets with the broken pieces of the five barley loaves which were left over after the people had eaten! (John 6:1-13, Phillips)

3

OUR MESSAGE

"You cain't give what you ain't got any more than you can come from where you ain't been." So spoke a wise old mountaineer. One might add, "Nor can you tell what you don't know!"

These few words embody the thrust of this chapter. To be a witness of God's grace (to others), you must first be a witness of God's grace (in your own life). To share, you must first possess. To tell, you must have prior knowledge.

Without acceptance of this fundamental fact, any discussion of witnessing is purely academic.

This truth, related to the nature of witnessing in another sphere, was vividly impressed upon me as a child of nine. But the lesson wasn't really learned until quite a number of years later.

Ross, a neighbor child from across the street, and I were playing on a swing hung on the cherry tree between our house and driveway. Our property fronted a busy provincial highway. Ross's brother, two and a half, was playing in our garden. Mother sat on the porch preparing vegetables for canning.

Suddenly, the scream of brakes pierced our quiet playtime. We looked to the highway. Skidding diagonally down the highway was a 1930 Ford, Model A, its broken bumper scraping sparks on the concrete. Before the car slid the broken body of little Calvin, lifeless even before tender hands picked it up.

Mother was summoned to an inquest into Calvin's death.

I remember asking, "But why do *you* have to go, Mamma?"

"Because I was the only witness to the accident." She had seen Calvin bound across the shoulder of the highway. The cry of warning stuck in her throat as she watched the horrified driver apply his brakes and turn the wheel. She saw the point of impact; she saw the broken bumper end drop to the concrete; she saw the little body thrown into the air, then fall sliding to the pavement; she saw the driver of the car rush to Calvin's side; she saw the anguished father stumble brokenly to the scene from his place of business across the street.

So she was called to be a witness at the inquest into Calvin's death.

Because she had been a witness she was called to be a witness. An absolute prerequisite to her appearance on the witness stand was her personal observation of the accident. Her own feelings and reactions to the tragedy were of no account at the court of inquiry. The judge insisted she limit her remarks to what she had seen and heard.

Her experience had constituted her a witness. It had become her only credential to give evidence. Without her firsthand involvement she would have had no right to speak; she would not have had the knowledge which validated her testimony.

WITNESSES FROM THE PAST

Three New Testament witnesses prescribe, in practice, a pattern of witness which fully supports the recognized definition of the word.

The Apostle Peter, with John, had seen the power of God, through their ministry, heal a man lame from his mother's womb. At the scene of the miracle, Peter spoke to the crowd.

"Ye men of Israel, why marvel ye at this? . . . The God of Abraham . . . hath glorified his Son Jesus; whom ye delivered up

. . . and killed the Prince of life, whom God hath raised from
dead; *whereof we are witnesses"* (Acts 3:12-15).

The religious leaders were baffled at the miracle and angry
at this recurrence of Jesus' name. So they placed Peter and John
in prison overnight. The next day "they called them, and commanded them not to speak at all nor teach in the name of Jesus.
But Peter and John answered and said unto them, Whether it be
right in the sight of God to hearken unto you more than unto
God, judge ye. For we cannot but speak the things *which we have
seen and heard"* (Acts 4:18-20).

Peter had witnessed the death of Christ, His resurrection, and
His miraculous revelation in power. He had personal experience
with the living Christ. This became the driving compulsion of
his life, and his message.

A second witness is John.

"That which was from the beginning, which we have heard,
which we have seen with our eyes, which we have looked upon,
and our hands have handled, of the Word of life; *(for the life was
manifested, and we have seen it, and bear witness,* and shew unto
you that eternal life, which was with the Father, and was manifested unto us;) *that which we have seen and heard declare we
unto you . . ."* (I John 1:1-3).

John had experienced intimate fellowship with Christ. The
life which had been with the Father had broken forth into the
experience of men, and John had participated in this wonderful
revelation. Seeing and experiencing, he bore witness.

Paul also takes the witness stand. He tells of his experience
on the Damascus road. Smitten down by a great light, ". . . he
fell to the earth, and heard a voice saying unto him, Saul, Saul,
why persecutest thou me? And he said, Who art thou, Lord? And
the Lord said, I am Jesus whom thou persecutest. . . . And he
trembling and astonished said, Lord, what wilt thou have me to
do" (Acts 9:4-6)?

"And last of all he was seen of me also, as of one born out of
due time" (I Corinthians 15:8).

"For though I be free from all men, yet have I made myself

servant unto all. . . . I am made all things to all men, that I might
by all means save some. And this I do for the gospel's sake. . ."
(I Corinthians 9:19, 22, 23).

The Apostle Paul stayed on the witness stand to his death.
He had experienced and experimented with the grace and power
of God. He never tired of telling about God's work in his own
life. This was his message.

Our message dare not be less. Nor can it ever be more.

THE PROCESS OF MESSAGE-BEARING

The Christian Church is always witnessing. In fact, every
Christian is always witnessing. However, the character of the
witness is not predetermined or automatic. Sometimes the message given forth is positive and constructive. Other times it is
negative and damaging.

It is not difficult to assume the message read by the world
when it observes in the church its dogmatisms, its heavy-handed
organization, its emphasis on buildings, its disunity and divisive-
ness. Nor is the message unclear when the lives of Christians
reflect pride, materialism, strife, jealousies, and hatred.

Unfortunately, too many Christians fail to recognize the
essential element of witness in everything they do. No aspect of
a person's life can escape contributing to the message communicated to every observer.

Every individual projects an image. Opinions of others
regarding that person are formed on the basis of the image. This
projected image is really a message which is being communicated.
Image and message are synonymous.

The Christian wants to communicate the message of the
Gospel. The painful question he must face, however, is: "What is
the nature of the message getting across to the people who see
me?"

The fact that message-bearing is going on all the time undercuts the viewpoint that consistently special efforts must be put
forth as well as that which tends to professionalize the witnessing
function. The special effort must be applied at the point of deter-

mining the "what" rather than the "whether." That we always witness to something is clear; what we are saying is the big question.

OUR MESSAGE TODAY IS CHRIST—AND HIS WORK IN US

"No man hath seen God at any time; the only begotten Son, which is in the bosom of the Father, he hath declared him" (John 1:18).

Jesus' mission to the world involved a declaration of what God was like. Not in word alone, but in every aspect of His life, Jesus revealed the character of God. He reflected His Father's love and compassion, His purity, His justice, His judgment of sin. He knew God; He was God. His mission and message were synonymous—to help men know God.

We have no other mission, or message. To help men know God is our prime concern. To bring men to see Jesus Christ as He revealed the Father. To reflect, in our own lives, His redeeming grace.

Our point of contact with the Father has been Jesus Christ and His Spirit. So we witness of Him. Our witness centers in Christ, not as in an object, but as the essence of our new life. By giving us spiritual aliveness, He has become the resource for our witness. He is our message.

His aliveness has become our aliveness. Indeed, this was the core of the disciples' testimony. From the first announcement at the tomb to this day, the disciples of Jesus have passed the glad word along from heart to heart, "He is not dead; He is risen." The resurrection of Jesus shattered the bonds of death, opened the door to eternal life for men and women, and since then constitutes the message of His followers. "Because I live, ye shall live also" (John 14:19).

The reality of aliveness pushes itself beyond the confines of private knowledge into the daylight of observable experience. The Christian can say, "I know Jesus lives because I see evidence of His life in me. I know this miracle is true because of what is happening to me daily."

The resurrection of Jesus from the dead is more than a note in history. It is more than a tenet of the Christian faith. It is more than a sentence in our creed. His resurrection, and the life which bursts forth from death, is an experiential fact—a part of personal experience. And so the witness shares the glad news, "In the midst of my death and among the dying, I have found life; I am finding life."

The witness continues, "Each day, in the circumstances that could crush me into oblivion, I find His life supporting me. His life throbs in my being. His divine nature, of which I am a blessed partaker, reflects itself in word and deed. His love and compassion course through my heart and love where I could not love; forgive where I could not forgive. He is alive; I see His life in me. His life is mine."

This is our message.

The work of Christ in our lives is more than a theological fact. It is more than a Scriptural theory. It is more than personal opinion or a private philosophy. It is an observable phenomenon, both subjective and objective in character. As witnesses, we teach the Gospel as it has been revealed to us. The reality of our experiential knowledge constitutes our testimony. The limit of our testimony is defined only by how fully Jesus Christ has become the answer to our needs.

Our message is not an argument (a man with experience is never at the mercy of a man with an argument); it is a report. We share information. John's Gospel, for example, was not written as a doctrinal treatise but rather as a testimony. Simplicity of presentation marks testimony as authentic. Heavy theological forms may signify scholarship but they often raise questions about the authenticity and down-to-earth quality of the experience.

Nor is our witness a recounting of what we have done—but of what Christ has done in us. Our terminology, and its focus, often confuses the issue. *We accept Christ; we have become new creatures; we are filled with the Spirit.* It is not so much our accepting Christ that is worthy of sharing—but the glorious truth that He has accepted us. The message is not that we love God—but that

He loved us. We do not tell of our new strength—but of His sufficiency.

What He has become to us, and is becoming, forms the substance of our message. Paul writes, "We warn everyone we meet, and we teach everyone we can, all that we know about him" (Colossians 1:28, Phillips). All that we know about Him is our testimony. To know little about Him is probably to sound unconvinced and uncertain, leaving a question mark in the mind of all who hear and observe. To know nothing about Him excludes us from the multitude of witnesses to His grace. We are witnesses only of what we have seen and heard.

THE MESSAGE MUST BE CURRENT

The only valid message is that with a current base. Many times, the question is asked, "What has Christ done for you?" The question should be, "What is Christ doing for you?"

Someone has said that the problem with a Christian's witness today is a matter of tenses. Many Christians can recount historical facts. They tell what Christ has accomplished. They speak of His incarnation, His death, His resurrection, and His ascension. Or they refer to the year and the month and the day of their personal encounter with Christ. Other times they speak of the future, Christ's return, and the bliss of heaven. But they seldom use the present tense.

Jesus said, "I am the way, the truth, and the life. . . ." He said also, "I am the bread of life." Not "I was" or "I will be." *I am.* Jesus speaks of the present. The witness for Christ will also speak of the present, of what the Lord is doing for him now.

This is what he tells others. One's testimony is like manna. It must be shared. It cannot be held without becoming a dead thing, decayed and putrid. It must be used, given away—or given up.

THE MESSAGE MUST BE GIVEN IN LOVE AND HUMILITY

God communicated His love for humanity in the gift of life through Christ. Jesus' ministry on earth—His healing of the sick,

His feeding of the multitudes, His teaching of the disciples—reflected loving concern. His death on the cross, as a sacrifice for sin, revealed the depth, the breadth, the intensity of that love. His intercessory work as Advocate with the Father confirms His love.

The intent and substance of God's message to mankind was love. This must also be true of every aspect of our witness. Without love, we deny the work of grace professed. Without love, we drain away the essence of our testimony. Without love, we leave hungry hearts with a stone. Without love, we make only a hollow sound. "If I were to speak with the combined eloquence of men and angels I should stir men like a fanfare of trumpets or the crashing of cymbals, but unless I had love, I should do nothing more. If I had the gift of foretelling the future and had in my mind not only all human knowledge but the secrets of God, and if, in addition, I had that absolute faith which can move mountains, but had no love, I tell you I should amount to nothing at all. If I were to sell all my possessions to feed the hungry and, for my convictions, allowed my body to be burned, and yet had no love, I should achieve precisely nothing" (I Corinthians 13:1-3, Phillips).

In one sense, we have no message of our own. We are but carriers of God's message to the world; channels through which flows the healing balm of His life. He continues to speak; He redeems still; He keeps on forgiving—all through us.

To recognize this should lead to an honest humility as we witness. The witnes stand is not raised above the multitudes. It is placed on the crowded pavement of life. The witness never speaks from a pedestal of perfection—but from the level of "We also are men of like passions with you . . ." (Acts 14:15).

The witness admits his humanness. Willingly, though sometimes painfully, he strips away the veneer and confesses his weaknesses, his temptations, his sins. He acknowledges personal problems. When he does this, the non-Christian will begin to identify. Self-sufficiency and self-righteousness build a wall which keeps the sinner at arm's length. But admission of humanness opens hearts.

This becomes the golden opportunity to share. Weaknesses—
yes, but new strength in Christ. Temptations—yes, but amazing
victory through faith in Him. Sins—yes, but a gracious forgiveness
in His name and a cleansing from all unrighteousness. Problems
—many of them, but as a child of God there are new insights as
well as a quiet confidence with which to face them, confidence
in a loving heavenly Father.

The true Christian never has confidence in his ability to
witness adequately. He has confidence only in the certain fact
that Jesus Christ has done something for him about which he
wants to speak. This confidence is not self-induced but reflects
simple assurance in the wonder of grace. And it does not have a
superior flavor.

There is no room for condescension in the life of the person
who has been delivered from the power of evil. No attitude of
supremacy. No spirit of superiority. All of us must be reminded
constantly that the new life in Jesus Christ is a gift and that none
of us have done anything to earn or deserve this gift. This spirit
of humility permeating the life of the Christian carries a great
impact. Essentially, it forms a part of the message.

The Message Must Be Translated

The need for translation in message-bearing is fulfilled in
two major ways. The first has to do with the content of the message which must be relevant to the experience norms of the hearer.

The Christian witness never forgets his own elemental needs
—those he shares with all other humans—the hungers, the fears,
the inner emptiness, the search for security. The witness acknowledges these same needs in his own life. He reports the truth about
himself, but then goes on to tell how Jesus Christ has provided
the answers. He can inform the hearer, from personal experience,
that God has come and continues to come to men and women
who are needy and helpless. He offers them fulfillment of life.
He grants them reconciliation with God and with each other. He
brings them hope which is both immediate and eternal.

The reporting aspect of witnessing cannot be overemphasized. In one sense, the witness stands back, almost as an impersonal observer, to tell about the work of the Spirit of God in his own life as well as the lives of his friends. Reporting eliminates the overbearing insistence that the hearer acquiesce; the discourteous coercion to a premature decision; the crude intrusions into the intimate chambers of personality. And incidentally, though significantly, reporting bypasses completely some of the reasons for the fears and frustrations fostered by an overemphasis on technique.

To witness is to report; to present the evidence growing out of personal experience. That is all!

The second point at which translation of the message must be kept in mind, in addition to relevant content, is the choice of words to convey content. The witness dare never forget that the average person to whom he speaks has shared neither his religious background nor his personal experience. The hearer may be totally ignorant of or thoroughly confused about the great truths in which Christians believe. More than that, he may not even care to know. At any rate, to begin speaking of sin or salvation or the new birth or the cross or the blood of Christ or justification or heaven or hell, without careful introduction or explanation and interpretation, only creates greater confusion. For all practical purposes, many of these words sound as if they came from a foreign language. Or at best, they have been invested with distorted and unbiblical meanings.

The message we bear must be shared in words common to everyday vocabulary. We speak simply of the reality within. Even though done in a stumbling manner, a witness is given. In fact, the lack of glib polish carries its own message. The hearer will sense the sincerity of our communication. And he will begin to open up because of this sincerity and because he senses that here is one who has obviously faced similar experiences in life.

The witness is not teaching doctrine; nor is he primarily sharing a set of facts. Having spoken to both content and the use of proper verbal symbols to convey content, one must go on to say that the definition of witness is fulfilled more adequately through relationship than by content. The ultimate in translation is reached not in the precision of words or in the correctness of doctrine but essentially in the quality of relationship.

Doctrine alone is never sufficient for witnessing. But the context in which the doctrine is set is important. Jesus related everything to life and the needs of individuals. He was not overly concerned with the transmission of a set of truths, but He was concerned about the real-life situation in which the individual found himself. He was concerned about the needs of the person. And because He was concerned about these needs, He did something about them. As He acted to meet needs, He also reflected doctrine, or a philosophy, or a certain viewpoint. But He was not primarily concerned whether the idea itself got across but rather that man's need was met.

Content, form, and relationship demand a language beyond the symbolic. Symbols must be concretized. Essence must be captured and brought to reality where the senses of men can perceive. This is what God did in Christ through the incarnation and on the cross. The message God wished to convey to mankind was reported in an unmistakable idiom when Jesus became flesh, dwelt among men, and died for them. No greater eloquence could have been conceived.

And no lesser language will meet the need for communication today.

The Messenger—The Message Incarnate

"And the Word was made flesh, and dwelt among us, (and we beheld his glory, the glory as of the only begotten of the Father,) full of grace and truth" (John 1:14).

God's language was the language of incarnation. He spoke to men through His Son Jesus. The message of God was not words spoken into the air or impressed on paper. It was the Word made flesh.

No more graphic language has yet been devised than that inherent in physical form and action. The deeds of men always bespeak a philosophy. They define in considerable detail and with great impact the thoughts of a mind. They uncover the hidden purposes and motivations, often in dramatic ways.

To discuss message in terms of a spoken witness covers only some of the necessary ground. The life itself conveys a message. Actions communicate. The messenger himself becomes the message. In short, every aspect of his life, including word and deed, constitutes the message being communicated. And back of all this is the essence of "being" from which resource every expression flows forth.

The Word must be made flesh in our lives. Jesus Christ, His way, His truth, His life, must become incarnate in us. His love, compassion, forgiveness, justice, purity, must be ours. They are ours as we become "partakers of the divine nature," as His life becomes ours.

Paul writes, "For in him dwelleth all the fulness of the Godhead bodily. And ye are complete in him" (Colossians 2:9, 10). His fullness is ours. Our completeness is in Him. As this grows into reality, our witness becomes increasingly a reflection of Him. This is how we witness of Jesus Christ. This is the content of our message—what He has done and continues to do in us.

The life of a witness is simply a Christlike life. It shows what God is like. It answers questions about the character of God. It reveals His nature.

Multitudes call for a certain word about God, about meaning in life, about redemption. If there is a God, they demand evidence. The Greeks said, "Sir, we would see Jesus" (John 12:21). Millions echo this cry. It is the privilege of Christian witnesses to show them a picture of Christ, a reflection of His life—in theirs.

Children think of God in relation to human beings they know, perhaps a father and grandfather. Many non-Christians are like children; they need a well-defined picture of God, a concrete illustration of divine power. The only concept of God they can understand is the one they see in the life of a Christian.

One of our concerns should be to give people a correct image of Christ. There is so much misunderstanding of who He is and what He does. Some of this misunderstanding arises out of ignorance and conjecture. Some has come from misrepresentation. The Christian witness exercises care in his life so that he truly represents his Lord. He is aware that everything he does, as a professing Christian, has a bearing on the conclusions people reach about God and Christ and Christianity.

The significance of the living image cannot be overemphasized. Even of Christ John wrote, "In him was life; and the life was the light of men." His life—all that He was, did, and said—constituted a way out of the darkness. His life was the light.

Sometimes an overconcern about witnessing as an activity leads us astray. The primary and basic concern of the Christian is simply to allow the life of Christ to permeate his being and consequently his doing. The life is the light. The light of Christ's life will be seen in everything he says and does. Witnessing is not really separate from living in function and experience. Witness is the result of a particular kind of life being lived before man and not a separate exercise to be engaged in as an option.

Christ, and His continuing work of redemption in us, is our message. Paul writes, "For we preach not ourselves, but Christ Jesus the Lord; and ourselves your servants for Jesus' sake. For God, who commanded the light to shine out of darkness, hath shined in our hearts, to give the light of the knowledge of the glory of God in the face of Jesus Christ" (II Corinthians 4:5, 6).

The life of Christ, in us, brings joy, gentleness, patience, trust—additional aspects of the message reflected in the life of the messenger. Joy in the Lord, in spite of external circumstances; gentleness and consideration of others; patience when plans are upset or unexpected problems develop; trust, a freedom from worry, in the face of great difficulties or overwhelming obstacles.

One could go on indefinitely listing the Christlike characteristics which constitute a witness to Him. But our purpose is not served by compiling a list of characteristics which become a standard against which we measure our life and witness. Rather, these few are mentioned to illustrate simply that all Christ has become to us goes to make up the message spoken by our lives.

And conversely, that part of our lives still not under His lordship also constitutes a part of the message, a negative part.

The Holy Spirit, living in us, longs to picture Christ to the world in all His beauty and power. This objective is thwarted whenever our yieldedness to the Spirit is less than complete. Then our witness of what Christ is may be imperfect, twisted, or incomplete. Nevertheless, it is a witness to what Christ has been able to do in our lives. Able to do, not because of inability on His part but rather because of lack of commitment on our part.

At one and the same time, this witness, distorted or limited though it may be, is a reflection of God's grace and an embarrassment to us for not allowing this grace to operate more fully in our hearts.

The messenger cannot be separated from his message. What he is, and therefore what he says and does, constitutes the witness which goes forth from his life. This can be both discouraging and heartening.

Paul wrote, "But we have this treasure in earthen vessels, that the excellency of the power may be of God, and not of us" (II Corinthians 4:7). The earthen vessels sometimes are cracked and misshapen. Yet the glory of God's grace is that it can be carried in and dispensed from these inadequate vessels. Thus God's power and glory are enhanced as ordinary men and women, inadequate and imperfect, but ready to be used, show forth and tell of God's wonderful greatness from a knowledge born of experience.

THE MESSENGER INTRODUCES

That the messenger introduces an individual to Christ could well be discussed under method. But it seems more appropriate to see this function as inherent in message.

The Christian has come to know Him, "whom to know is life eternal." He has found answers to some questions and is finding still more. He now sees meaning in life. He has been relieved of the heavy burden of guilt. He has experienced forgiveness and freedom and direction. He has uncovered insights regarding himself and relationships to others. He has discovered fellowship

—blessed release from aloneness.

He knows there is much to learn. But he recognizes that his present blessings in Christ have come to him because of his simple faith in Jesus Christ, the Son of God. Christ Himself has become new life, redeemed the past, and planted hope. Christ has become a new center for life. Christ has become the essence of being, the resource for every need, the nearest friend.

He has become the dearest treasure—a treasure to be shared.

The sharing is not a mechanical exercise. Rather, his changed life constitutes the witness. His new being issues in speech and deeds reflecting the massive difference between "before" and "after." The "reporting" of this change is going on all the time —every time he is with people.

As the impact of this reporting "sinks in," questions are asked. Doors are opened. Opportunities to share more explicitly are provided.

Then the witness can introduce his friend, the great life-changer. But if he's wise, he will only introduce Him. Just as a forced introduction results often in unpleasantness, so a forced acquaintance is shrugged off as quickly as possible. The person introduced must move toward his own firsthand relationship with Christ if there is to be any lasting validity to the introduction.

This is his choice!

As he thinks on his observations of the evidence, listens to testimony, and weighs the alternatives, he may well ask more questions. The Christian's message of witness will come through in every answer. In fact, every step in the encounter and dialogue contributes to the introduction. As the Holy Spirit works, in many ways, the hearer will be nudged gently toward decision. He cannot escape. If he postpones, the gentle nudge becomes a crushing pressure, until he answers. But this is the Spirit's work—not man's.

Mere man is not in the soul-winning business. His commission is not to win souls or convert people. Without denying that the Christian witness is a necessary link in God's chain of love, it must be emphasized that the conversion of a man is the work

of the Holy Spirit. The Christian cannot even share his faith in
Jesus Christ; that is, he cannot transfer it to another. He reports
the evidence; he informs of his experience; he introduces those
he meets to the Saviour.

What happens then is a responsibility shared by God and the
individual who has been brought face to face with Christ—in the
life of one of His messengers.

"You cain't give what you ain't got. . . ."

To give demands prior possession. To share requires discovery of a resource. To introduce presupposes acquaintance. In
addition to the story preceding this chapter, two others illustrate
these obvious principles.

"And there were four leprous men at the entering in of the
gate: and they said one to another, Why sit we here until we
die? If we say, We will enter into the city, then the famine is in
the city, and we shall die there: and if we sit still here, we die also.
Now therefore come, and let us fall unto the host of the Syrians:
if they save us alive, we shall live; and if they kill us, we shall but
die. And they rose up in the twilight, to go unto the camp of the
Syrians: and when they were come to the uttermost part of the
camp of Syria, behold, there was no man there. For the Lord had
made the host of the Syrians to hear a noise of chariots, and a
noise of horses, even the noise of a great host: and they said one
to another, Lo, the king of Israel hath hired against us the kings
of the Hittites, and the kings of the Egyptians, to come upon us.
Wherefore they arose and fled in the twilight, and left their tents,
and their horses, and their asses, even the camp as it was, and fled
for their life. And when these lepers came to the uttermost part
of the camp, they went into one tent, and did eat and drink, and
carried thence silver, and gold, and raiment, and went and hid
it; and came again, and entered into another tent, and carried
thence also, and went and hid it. Then they said one to another,
We do not well: this day is a day of good tidings, and we hold our
peace: if we tarry till the morning light, some mischief will come
upon us: now therefore come, that we may go and tell the king's
household. So they came and called unto the porter of the city:

and they told them, saying, We came to the camp of the Syrians, and, behold, there was not man there, neither voice of man, but horses tied, and asses tied, and the tents as they were. And he called the porters; and they told it to the king's house within" (II Kings 7:3-11).

The leprous beggars found food and brought the good report to the starving city.

"And they came over unto the other side of the sea, into the country of the Gadarenes. And when he was come out of the ship, immediately there met him out of the tombs a man with an unclean spirit, who had his dwelling among the tombs; and no man could bind him, no, not with chains: because that he had been often bound with fetters and chains, and the chains had been plucked asunder by him, and the fetters broken in pieces: neither could any man tame him. And always, night and day, he was in the mountains, and in the tombs, crying, and cutting himself with stones. But when he saw Jesus afar off, he ran and worshipped him, and cried with a loud voice, and said, What have I to do with thee, Jesus, thou Son of the most high God? I adjure thee by God, that thou torment me not. For he said unto him, Come out of the man, thou unclean spirit. And he asked him, What is thy name? And he answered, saying, My name is Legion: for we are many. And he besought him much that he would not send them away out of the country. Now there was there nigh unto the mountains a great herd of swine feeding. And all the devils besought him, saying, Send us into the swine, that we may enter into them. And forthwith Jesus gave them leave. And the unclean spirits went out, and entered into the swine: and the herd ran violently down a steep place into the sea, (they were about two thousand;) and were choked in the sea. And they that fed the swine fled, and told it in the city, and in the country. And they went out to see what it was that was done.

"And they come to Jesus, and see him that was possessed with the devil, and had the legion, sitting, and clothed, and in his right mind: and they were afraid. And they that saw it told them how it befell to him that was possessed with the devil, and also concerning the swine. And they began to pray him to depart out of their coasts. And when he was come into the ship, he that had been possessed with the devil prayed him that he might be with him. Howbeit Jesus suffered him not, but saith unto him, Go home to thy friends, and tell them how great things the Lord hath done for thee, and hath had compassion on thee" (Mark 5:1-19).

The demon-possessed man met Jesus Christ. As a result, he was directed to tell his friends what God had done for him.

Message implies an interesting cycle. It comes to man through proclamation in one form or another. God's grace, the heart of the message, leads to reconciliation. The sinner, reconciled, finds God's life present in his life—grace and love personified or expressed in word and deed. In turn, this new life becomes the message proclaimed to still others, completing the cycle.

"You cain't give what you ain't got. . . ." But what is yours in Christ can be shared. This is your message.

Christ began with the relevant—

There he came to a little town called Sychar, which is near the historic plot of land that Jacob gave to his son, Joseph, and "Jacob's Spring" was there. Jesus, tired with the journey, sat down beside it, just as he was. The time was about midday. Presently, a Samaritan woman arrived to draw some water.

"Please give me a drink," Jesus said to her, for his disciples had gone away to the town to buy food. The Samaritan woman said to him, "How can you, a Jew, ask for a drink from me, a woman of Samaria?" (For Jews have no dealings with Samaritans.)

"If you knew what God can give," Jesus replied, "and if you knew who it is that said to you, 'Give me a drink,' I think you would have asked him, and he would have given you living water!"

"Sir," said the woman, "you have nothing to draw water with and this well is deep—where can you get your living water? Are you a greater man than our ancestor, Jacob, who gave us this well, and drank here himself with his family, and his cattle?"

Jesus said to her, "Everyone who drinks this water will be thirsty again. But whoever drinks the water I will give him will never be thirsty again. For my gift will become a spring in the man himself, welling up into eternal life."

The woman said, "Sir, give me this water, so that I may stop being thirsty—and not have to come here to draw water any more!"

* * *

So the woman left her water pot behind and went into the town and began to say to the people, "Come out and see the man who told me everything I've ever done! Can this be 'Christ'?" So they left the town and started to come to Jesus.

* * *

Many of the Samaritans who came out of that town believed in him through the woman's testimony—"He told me everything I've ever done." And when they arrived they begged him to stay with them. He did stay there two days, and far more believed in him because of what he himself said. As they told the woman: "We don't believe any longer now because of what you said. We have heard him with our own ears. We know now that this must be the man who will save the world!" (John 4:5-15, 28-30, 39-42, Phillips)

4

OUR METHOD

Message and method are practically inseparable. They form two sides of the same coin. To speak of one is to imply the other. A discussion of either appears to overlap at many points. Any attempt at separation for purposes of definition and clarity should not be seen as a contradiction to this close integration.

Of course, a purely mechanical or more professional view of witnessing could allow for a simple delineation between message content and technique of approach and presentation. If witnessing is only an exercise, then technique takes on a different hue.

However, in these pages, an effort will be made to show that no man lives unto himself. The sum total of an individual's life leaves a continuing influence of one kind or another. Every aspect of personality expressed outwardly in any form projects an image and carries a message. This basic principle of human interrelationship provides the foundation for the thrust of this entire manuscript.

This chapter, therefore, is not a description of a new method or an announcement of exciting discoveries of unknown witness patterns. It simply supports the idea that an understanding of the term "witness" shows the experience to be a natural part of

3

Christian living. Witnessing is *being* the person God has calle
me to be. Witnessing is being oneself before others, the new sel
in Christ Jesus, a self controlled by the Holy Spirit. Witnessin
is reflecting a way of life, sharing a pattern for living.

Our witness has to do with a person. The message reflecte
in word and deed points always to Christ. Consequently, there i
no one right way to introduce Him to people. No one metho
that may be promoted to the exclusion of others. No last wor
except that which grows out of each Christian's witnessing exper
ence as the Spirit leads him.

Probably most "methods" would fall into two categories—th
direct and indirect approach. Both are Scriptural. Both hav
been abused, largely because they have been misunderstood. I
this context of misunderstanding and abuse, they appear to b
opposing viewpoints. In actual fact, they are related to each othe

The indirect approach recognizes that every aspect of lif
contributes to the essence of Christian witness. The direc
approach acknowledges that there are times when the Holy Spiri
leads an alert Christian to a heart already prepared for a specifi
question regarding spiritual welfare or a clear invitation to com
to Christ.

The abuse of the indirect approach usually lies in the conclu
sion that speaking about Christ is unnecessary or out of place
Nothing is further from the truth. Speech is as much a part o
normal living as is walking. The abuse of the direct approach i
usually seen in a boldness born of the flesh which glibly spouts
sequence of words and phrases from a private vocabulary, quie
insensitive to either the gentle nudgings or quiet restraints of th
Spirit of God.

The real problem has grown out of an unwarranted promo
tion of the direct approach as *the* method, of seeing soul-winnin
as a necessary exercise, and of an unfortunate implication tha
unsaved persons are little digits to be pushed from one column t
the next so that another gold star can be added to the "soul
winner's" report card. These attitudes, often assumed but seldom
expressed, have brought the Christian witness into disrepute. An

consequently, in its narrowest sense, witnessing has been reduced to the level of an optional activity.

Perhaps these lines can provide perspective from which to view this essential aspect of Christian living. Having acknowledged the place of direct confrontation, major emphasis here will be given to the framework of personal contact within which every aspect of life is seen as constituting a witness.

It Worked in the Apostle's Experience

The sequence of events in Chapter 1 of John's Gospel (verses 29-42) illuminates dramatically the simplicity of witness when it is recognized as the giving of evidence.

John the Baptist had been called to serve as a forerunner to Jesus. His commission from God had included a sign so that he would recognize the Messiah. When that sign was revealed—the Spirit descending like a dove on Jesus of Nazareth—John reports, "And I saw, and bare record that this is the Son of God" (verse 34).

Notice the two elements of this experience—"saw and bare record." Each is an essential element in witness. To see (witness) precedes bearing record (witnessing). The experience precedes the giving of evidence.

The following day, John again witnessed to that which he knew as fact. "And looking upon Jesus as he walked, he saith, Behold the Lamb of God" (verse 36)! This time two of John's disciples standing with him heard John speak and followed Jesus.

The drama of encounter had begun! Jesus looked around at them and asked what they were looking for. They asked Him where He lived. Jesus answered, "Come and see" (verse 39). They did and spent the day with Jesus.

"One of the two which heard John speak, and followed him, was Andrew, Simon Peter's brother. He first findeth his own brother Simon, and saith unto him, We have found the Messias, which is, being interpreted, the Christ. And he brought him to Jesus . . ." (verses 40-42).

Note again the steps in this chain of sharing. John witnessed a sign confirming the Messiah-ship of Jesus of Nazareth. He then shared his faith that this man was indeed the Christ. Of the two who heard him and spent time with Jesus, one, Andrew, evidently also now convinced in his own heart, reports his find to his brother Peter and brings him to Jesus.

A second drama in the same chapter (verses 43-46) confirms the pattern. Philip, called by Jesus to follow Him, came to believe in Him as the Christ. "Philip findeth Nathanael, and saith unto him, We have found him, of whom Moses in the law, and the prophets, did write, Jesus of Nazareth, the son of Joseph" (verse 45). Philip simply reported his conclusion regarding Jesus. He searched out Nathanael, undoubtedly a close friend, and shared his new belief, his faith. He had met Jesus, and reached a certain conclusion regarding Him. Now he shared this conclusion with another person.

But the story doesn't end here. Nathanael, for whatever reason, was skeptical. "Can there any good thing come out of Nazareth?"

This comment of doubt provided the opening for the only answer the Christian witness can ever give. "Come and see." Philip did not argue. Nor can today's witness argue. He simply presents his own testimony. Then, for every question, to every doubt, in the face of every skepticism, there is only one response— at once a challenge and an invitation—come and see!

A third illustration of simplicity in witness is found also in the Gospel of John (4:1-42). Here the Master Himself reflects a lesson whose impact is lost so often because it is so uncomplicated and common. In this case, a witness is given to a stranger, rather than to a friend. But the context of friendship is established immediately.

This person—a woman, a Samaritan, apparently morally lax —normally would have been the last individual a respectable Jewish gentleman would have considered addressing, and that in a public place. Yet Jesus at once accepted her as a person, acknowledged to her a need of His own, and opened a conversation entirely in keeping with the circumstances.

"Give me to drink."

Just a simple request. In these words there is no hint of condemnation or condescension, no suggestion of argument, no breath of religious insistence. And there is no flower of theology, although the seed is there as it is, indeed, in much of conversation.

Against the background of complete acceptance and out of an ordinary request for a drink of water grew a decision that uncovered the woman's need and pointed to an answer. She accepted the answer and very naturally chose to report her discovery to those whom she knew best.

From that report came a single result by two roads. Some of the Samaritans believed on the basis of the evidence she had given. Others ". . . believed because of his own word; and said unto the woman, Now we believe, not because of thy saying: for we have heard him ourselves, and know that this is indeed the Christ, the Saviour of the world" (verses 41, 42).

The result—". . . many of the Samaritans of that city believed on him for the saying of the woman . . ." and "many more believed because of his own word . . ."—hinged on two factors. The first was Jesus' simple approach of friendship; the second was the sharing of evidence by the woman. The essence of the Christian witness is nowhere more adequately pictured.

It Works in the World Today

Two personal experiences illustrate further the natural, almost unexpected, way in which a witness may be given. These are selected, among many, not because they show witness in the context of long friendship, but because they marked the revelation of new insights regarding the nature of witnessing. The same basic principles apply in a neighborhood or friendship context; in fact, their application there, in "normal" circumstances, is more likely to bear fruit than in a transient situation.

At one point in life, I was driving a milk transport to earn my living. One evening, the truck needed a small maintenance job; so I stopped at the dealer service agency where a truck mechanic was assigned to do the job. Although I had seen the man before, there was never time for more than a friendly "hello" in passing.

In the course of his work, the mechanic struck his thumb with an eight-pound machine hammer. He pushed the dolly out from under the truck chassis, jumped to his feet, and clutched his thumb. Then with a burst of feeling, although he hadn't uttered a word of profanity, he said, "That would make a preacher swear."

My immediate response, less thoughtful than sharp, was, "I doubt it."

He turned on me, partly in anger. "What do you know about it?"

Obviously missing the main point, but still in a lighter mood, I said, "I'm a preacher, and I don't feel like swearing."

He let go his thumb. "You're a preacher! Why in the world are you driving a milk truck?"

In the course of my answer, in which I mentioned the normal need to earn a living, I also told him of my faith in Christ and how it had led me to the ministry as a form of Christian service.

Six months later, he told me of his own newfound faith which had come to him in the midst of desperate need. Because he was an alcoholic, his children had been taken out of the home by a welfare agency. His wife had left him. He had lost his job. In a drunken depression he stumbled along the street of a small Canadian town. His wandering brought him up to a street meeting. A kindly Salvation Army major was sensitive to his plight and talked to him about his need and the answers the Lord could provide. Finally, he knelt on the curb and accepted Christ.

"Do you know why I did it?" he asked me. "Remember the time I hit my thumb?"

I nodded.

"Remember you took a minute or two to tell me why you were a Christian?"

I nodded again.

"That stuck. I couldn't forget it. One other person did the same. Your words kept coming back to me when I didn't know what to do anymore. Then the Lord used the major to put the touch on me. But those testimonies softened me up. I was ready."

As he spoke, the light of insight seemed to dawn in my mind. I had witnessed, although at the time I thought I had failed because I had failed to invite the man to accept Christ. For years, through adolescence and into my early ministry, I had carried a major impression—every man I met was my personal responsibility to win to Christ. Many times I tried to speak and failed. Other times I struggled through a feeble paragraph but seldom reached the point of inviting the person to become a Christian.

The sense of failure and frustration was overwhelming, until suddenly I realized it was not really my job to convert men and women, but simply to tell them what the Lord had done for me. Drawing a soul to Christ was the work of the Holy Spirit.

Sometime later I was in summer school at a Canadian university. One noontime, in the cafeteria line, a young man turned to me and said, "Mind if we eat together?"

"Certainly not," I said.

We talked of many things during the meal, none of them religious in nature, all of them forgotten except one.

As we finished our dessert, he put his elbows on the table, folded his hands, and said, "What's wrong with you?"

I'm sure I blinked at the abruptness of the question. That there was reason to ask the question may be obvious to most. But such bluntness did seem a bit out of place.

"Why?" I asked as soon as I got over the initial shock.

"We've been sitting here talking for twenty minutes and you haven't used one word of profanity."

My first reaction was to make a few comments about people whose English vocabulary was so impoverished that they were forced to resort to profanity. But the thought came to me immediately, *This isn't the real reason.*

So I said simply, "God is my Father and Jesus Christ is my Saviour. And I can't bring myself to use their names in a profane way."

He nodded for me to go on. I did, giving my testimony of faith in Christ and what this had meant in my life. Later, in meditating on the encounter, I was suddenly impressed with the fact that a witness had been given. But again this ran counter to my previous conclusion that the button-holing, doorbell-ringing, are-you-a-Christian approach was the only way.

Several fundamental points stood out. I hadn't asked for this contact—evidently the Spirit of God had arranged it. I had only been myself—this had constituted a witness. I had answered a question honestly—as a Christian, not just as a lover of the English language without profane embellishments.

Since then, again and again, in travel and at home, I have found opportunities to respond as a Christian to requests for help, to questions that cried out for answers, to situations that called for a sharing of what I had or knew. The Lord seems to prepare hearts, then leads one to the spot where a smile, a kind word, a helping hand, a sharing of one's faith seem to be the most natural thing in the world—because of the spirit of Christ. To watch for these openings has become an exciting adventure and a real source of joy in the Christian life.

ANALYSIS OF METHOD

The dissection of an organism usually presupposes the death of the organism. To dissect the methodology of witness and discern its essence without cutting into its obvious dynamic is difficult, to say the least, if not impossible. Yet the process of learning may take place best when each element is studied carefully, then assimilated into one's own being through experience which reflects the lessons learned. In this context, we shall attempt an analysis of method which can move the reader toward this objective.

At least three factors are present in any witnessing situation: time, place, relationship. The first two, although significant, may be dealt with summarily; the last calls for careful delineation. Actually, time and place are always involved in relationship.

1. *Time.* Time is life. That is, time is a measurement device

which shows the passage of a life through a small segment of eternity (if the words "time" and "segment" can ever be used within the context of eternity). In other words, minutes and hours and days represent portions of a life.

Christians speak of dedicating their lives to Christ. They mean by this directing the concerns of their minds, the energies of their bodies, the consecutive parts of their lives, called hours and days and months and years, into channels of usefulness, so determined by the plan of God.

God's primary and ultimate concern is the redemption of men and women to Himself. Although in one sense Jesus Christ completed His Father's redemptive work on the cross, in another sense He only began it. That is to say, God continues to love men in a redeeming manner through the body of Christ, the church.

There are two ways to speak of God's redeeming work through the church. On the one hand, it is carried out through the lives of members of that body. On the other hand, one could say there is no redemption without death, and that the body is offered up continuously not as atonement in the sense of Christ's offering, but nevertheless in a continuing practical demonstration of God's sacrificial love to all men.

So the member of the body of Christ, committing himself to Christ, literally offers his life to redeem individuals. This is not a theological fantasy but a hard reality. To be a part of Christ's body is to be intimately and inescapably involved in the concerns of Christ. It is to feel the throb of His compassionate heart. It is to reach out in mercy and grace. It is literally to have Him extend us into the needs of human beings. It is to see our very life—hours and days—spent in the great and divine effort to reveal God's love to the world.

There is no limit to the amount of time we allot to this redeeming process. All of life for Christ allows for no reservations. No hour in the day can escape the demand that it be redemptive in character. No portion of a life is held back. Commitment of life to Christ means literally the commitment of time to His purposes. To accept Jesus Christ as Saviour is to accept a new vocation—His vocation—the loving of men and women.

The Christian witness considers himself expendable—spendable. He invests the currency of his life in a reflection of God's love, so that others may find eternal value. He actually gives his life, as did Christ, to announce the love of Christ.

The cross announced the love of God in unmistakable tones. In this way also, the sacrifice of a life proclaims a love in language that may puzzle in terms of motivation but is always clear in terms of content.

This sacrifice is a death—death to self. A daily dying so that life may issue forth. Jesus said, "Verily, verily, I say unto you, Except a corn of wheat fall into the ground and die, it abideth alone: but if it die, it bringeth forth much fruit. He that loveth his life shall lose it; and he that hateth his life in this world shall keep it unto life eternal" (John 12:24, 25).

This is the essence of our gift to others, and thus to Christ. Without time—literal hours—relationship is an impossibility. Theoretically, we may conclude there are other things we can give. But time is fundamental. And in the offering of time we begin truly to offer ourselves.

There is a kind of photograph called a time exposure. The impression of a scene or a situation or even movement on sensitized photographic paper in a time exposure can produce interesting results. The same is true in life.

Individuals need a time exposure to Christ—in us. This kind of exposure can change lives, as we ourselves can testify. To be in the presence of Christ as reflected in the life of a believer should be a refreshing experience. And this is our call—to make available to those searching for an honest picture of life a time exposure of Jesus Christ.

This takes time. This calls for hours spent. This costs a life.

This is witnessing.

As noted above, there is no limit to the amount of time we allot to this redemptive work. It is an integral part of our life, woven into the warp and woof of our spiritual being. Yet there is a practical limit which must be recognized.

Later we will look at the servant role of the witness. To assume servanthood for persons implies definite limitations. The servant cannot do good work by serving a thousand masters; the witness cannot serve best by knocking on one thousand doors but rather by getting to know one or several persons or families well. Only in this way can an honest interest be expressed and sincere friendship develop.

The effective witness, even though all his time is literally given to Christ, by design will restrict the number of intimate contacts. No one of us has enough time to reach every individual. By spreading ourselves too thinly we undercut the impact of our lives and many times actually distort the message we are seeking to give.

We may meet some persons many times in the course of regular activity. These we come to know quite well. Others will remain superficial acquaintances. Out of all our contacts, especially those in the first group, there will likely be a few with whom there is repeated and natural interaction. In this context our witness is given most spontaneously and with the most pointed impact.

This was Christ's pattern. He limited Himself generally to a comparatively small group of people. Within this group there was the inner circle of disciples as well as a small number of intimate friends. Of course, beyond this circle He was always interested in the individual, but the time He had allotted to Him seemed to be focused quite sharply on a very limited group. To some, materialistically minded, this may seem like poor stewardship of time. In reality, to communicate with persons in depth is the only proper way to invest our limited time resources.

2. *Place.* Place refers to location. Also to vocation. Being creatures composed of physical matter, instead of spirit alone, we relate to the created world in which we live in terms of geography. Circumstances of birth, parental decisions, personal inclinations, politics, economic pressures, societal or cultural movements, conspire to locate us at one place or another.

In some countries placement at birth determines one's entire future. In others, like our own, personal initiative regarding location is a determinant of great influence. Here, theoretically at least, no one is forced to remain in one place all his life.

The same is true of vocation, a variant in the definition of place. Factors of aptitude and acquired skills being equal, a great deal of latitude in the choice of vocation is allowed the average individual in North America. Preparation or experience in any major field of study opens a variety of vocational possibilities to the average individual.

In the final analysis, there is probably no location and comparatively few vocations closed to the Christian. This means that Christians may be found and are to be found practically everywhere, geographically and vocationally. The implications of this fact to the mission of the church in this country are overwhelming. With a few notable exceptions, the same is true throughout the world.

Unfortunately, many Christians have overlooked the missionary potential in the geographical and vocational elements present in the church. Instead, mission boards have been organized, outreach programs have been set up, and individuals have been sent great distances to fulfill a mission whose major resource lies untouched. That resource is the multitude of professing Christians scattered around the world in practically every place—location and vocation.

For a variety of reasons, this army has not been mobilized. Indeed, most of its members are not even aware of the war. They are ignorant of objectives. They know nothing of strategy. They do not see their own obligation to witness of God's grace. And, sadly, in too many cases, they have little or nothing to say: God's power and grace have not yet touched and transformed them.

At one time, it seems as if the primary way in which the Gospel was spread into new parts of the world was through the migration of independent Christians who left their homes for one reason or another—business, family, adventure. Of course, in the early church, many left their homes because of persecution.

However, regardless of the reason for migration and settlement in a new region, it was this group of ordinary people, Christians, that formed a witnessing nucleus in the new communities of which they were becoming a part. These were truly the missionaries of that day. Actually, the Apostle Paul and his few close co-workers were exceptions to the rule.

In our day, we have taken the exception and made it the rule. Missionaries are usually thought of as those who are specially called and sent great distances by a sponsoring agency to do the work of witnessing. The rank and file support these programs, blithely assuming this token involvement fulfills their responsibility to the world of unsaved. Consequently, Christian leaders are forced constantly to decry the great untouched task and call for more workers. Obviously, there is a need for more workers. But who are they to be? Vast increments to the staff of present mission agencies? Or should the call rather go to the great army of the uninvolved in every location and vocation?

Specialization in Christian service, while deserving a certain place, has become a curse to the church. Special calls, appointments, and assignments have developed a false philosophy of mission. And they have contributed measurably to the misunderstanding and frustration regarding witnessing. The laying on of hands or the formal sending is not a prerequisite to witness.

Home base for witnessing, for most Christians, is simply the community in which they live. Every neighborhood provides an opportunity to reflect Christ—to the family next door, at the shopping center, at PTA meetings, at the place of employment, in telephone conversations, to the salesman making a call. Not a sermon, but a reflection of Christ—in attitude, tone of voice, facial expression, action, and word. The Christian enjoys what many of these individuals need, although they may not be able to define their need and although many Christians do not realize the worth of the blessings they possess in Christ.

The effective Christian witness is given right out in the mainstream of life, where individual meets individual, where working and living are going on, where the problems are real, and where the suffering is intense. This is where the impact of the Christian message can be felt. This is where the ministry of reconciliation can go on. This sphere of personal contact is where witnessing can be spontaneous, flexible, decentralized, and consequently relevant and meaningful.

To insist on formal programs of mission and witness ignores those areas in the world where this is impossible. It would seem logical to assume that God's work of redemption is not dependent on the well-organized methods to which we have become accustomed.

Dr. Smolick of Czechoslovakia reports on evangelism behind the iron curtain where the usual Western patterns of witness are impossible—renting a hall, preaching over the radio, and mass literature distribution. But, he says, when a Christian works in a factory alongside others, no government in the world can stop a Christian from loving his fellow worker; from reacting like Christ in difficult situations; from living his personal life in a way that is different and becomes a light to those who observe. This is the kind of Christian witness that works in every context, even behind the iron curtain. And, one might add, there should be no need of an iron curtain to confirm the validity of this approach to witness.

With rare exceptions, place—location and vocation—puts us into proximity with individuals. We are a part of society. Relationship with others is an integral part of social interaction. This is the third factor to which we direct our attention in the analysis of method.

3. *Relationship.* The connecting line between individuals, upon which relationship is based, varies infinitely. Location and vocation are perhaps the most obvious. Usually location is, or has been, a prime element in the establishment of relationship. However, within the context of relative physical proximity, an unnumbered host of other factors contribute measurably to the extent of relationship between people.

Family, temperament, intellect, personal interests, politics, economics merely symbolize the major influences which bear upon individuals and help to determine the kind and quality of their relationship with each other.

The Christian is subject to all these influences in a similar manner unless he isolates himself in one way or another. Sometimes these influences are seen as threats. Then the misdirected concern leads to a withdrawal from the social community. And the channel for relationships is short-circuited.

On the other hand, the alert disciple of Christ sees this situation as a blessing. He is not unaware of the dangers. In fact, he recognizes that even the incarnation of Christ was a risk. He knows that as Christ becomes flesh in his own experience, he will be exposing himself to a similar risk. He does it anyway, for Jesus' sake, and in His strength.

An effective witness is never given at arm's length. This fact does not negate the values of seed-sowing forms of service, the public preaching of the Word, or the use of literature. It only emphasizes the centrality of the personal element in witness. Relationship to individuals is the only realm within which the influence of a life can make an impact on human need.

When that point is recognized, another question still remains: How can the Christian move into relationship with non-Christians in a way that will honor Christ and reflect the desired witness of what His grace and power can accomplish? This may be answered briefly by listing the sequence of experience which leads to relationship. Then we shall move on to look at each one separately: acquaintance, acceptance, dialogue, friendship, identification, involvement, servanthood, suffering, death!

a. Acquaintance. The elementary step of acquaintance is so obvious that it should not need to be mentioned. But it is so basic and so often ignored that to bypass it would be to confirm the error of countless Christians. These live the years away without any attempt to enlarge their circle of acquaintance among non-Christians. As a result, they can never really move beyond themselves into outreach for Christ because this is the only bridge leading to the other aspects of involvement which constitute witness.

The Christian witness *must* become acquainted with the non-Christian. He must learn to know people personally. Different kinds of people. In some degree, he must become familiar with the circumstances in which they live, their reaction to various problems, their motivations for decision and action, their philosophies of life.

This requires more than a knowledge of the mass or an intellectual awareness of the universal problems which plague the person without faith in Christ. This demands more than insight into human nature, an understanding of sociological laws, or the principles of mass psychology.

The Christian witness must become acquainted, not with *the* non-Christian, but with *a* non-Christian. A specific person with a definitive name and distinctive features and a set of problems all his own. Not only one, but a number of such persons. The focus must be on the individual, however. Always! Not the group—the individual.

Acquaintance grows out of contact. To be sure, this is often casual, at first. Contact at the grocery store, at the service station, in community groups, at work, in school, through a helping hand given *or* received; almost anywhere—wherever there are people. Many times the Christian can turn a first casual contact into a second. Sometimes he need only respond to an overture from the other person.

Of course, great sensitivity is an asset here. Some people seem to keep everyone away from themselves. They do not wish to go beyond the formalities of polite interchange. Perhaps they have been hurt badly in previous encounters and are reluctant to risk the possibility of other disappointments. Or they may be bitter and resentful. Or they may not know how to respond.

In other cases, the signals which some individuals send, hinting at a desire for acquaintance, are so weak only the alert person will catch them. These are usually timid and often lonely because they can never take the first step toward acquaintance.

The Christian witness need not be overly concerned about the kinds of people he will meet. His first concern will be that every aspect of his life will be Christlike in character. Secondly, he must be ready to pay the price, in time or interest or helpfulness, to carry the casual contact, repeated or unexpected, to the level of acquaintance—reasonable familiarity with. Finally, he must be prepared to walk a long road. For acquaintance is only the bridge to useful service. When crossed, it represents but the first step in his commitment to be a faithful witness for Jesus Christ.

b. Acceptance. Immediately upon crossing the bridge of acquaintance, the Christian witness faces the formidable barrier of acceptance. Perhaps nothing blocks a witness so effectively as the inability to convey a sense of acceptance to the new acquaintance.

Christians are peculiarly adept at rejection, or at least the implication of rejection. Much of this is understandable, though not justified. In many cases, they have been born into Christian families. Their environment and teaching have led to an abhorrence of certain practices or activities. Sometimes, unfortunately, a self-righteous attitude develops. Everyone outside of the sacrosanct circle is looked down upon. The person is often rejected right along with his sinful habits and vices.

Acquaintance, within this context, is extremely difficult. Acceptance is practically impossible.

Or the new Christian, without a long spiritual heritage, has come into a wonderful freedom through faith in Christ. He senses forgiveness. He revels in the release from guilt. He is alive to the Spirit's leading in his life. He thrills to the experience of victory over sin. Sometimes the devil twists all of this into pity and condescension as the Christian looks back at the sodden pleasures of his former friends. And condescension slices acceptance into slivers that needle its object and drive him away.

The Christian, serious about the business of witnessing, will accept every person at face value. He will guard against prejudice toward an individual. He will seek to keep an open mind.

However, after all this is said and done, real acceptance demands another step. When, through acquaintance, he discovers a character which is repulsive, or seems to justify prejudice; or he observes behavior which cries out for reaction; or he experiences unkindness or slights directed at him—he will still be accepting in attitude. Without a doubt, this is a strenuous test. But if a witness is to reach through and touch that life, the test must be met through Gods grace.

Grace, in operation, reflects at least two dimensions. In the first place, the Christian remembers that God's undeserved favor came to him at a time when his own character and life had no merit in themselves. What he is and has now has not come to him as a result of personal merit or great effort. Secondly then, because of grace's work *in* his life, he has opened himself to a ministry of God's grace *through* his life. He has become a channel for grace to flow to other persons—similarly underserving of favor.

Jesus proved the point of acceptance over and over. Matthew at the seat of customs, He called to follow Him. Impulsive Peter and his crude fishermen friends, He graced with the name of disciples. Zacchaeus the thief, Mary Magdalene, the woman taken in adultery—upon each one He conferred the honor of acceptance. Just as they were. Without condemnation, or censure, or even implied rebuke.

They were persons. Persons in need. He had come to be their Saviour. Every word and action directed toward them was redemptive in character. He accepted them fully as they were. In this acceptance, they found warmth and love and the courage to look at themselves. And the strength to let His life change them.

Contrast this with the judgment Christians are prone to flood over the broken hearts and the bruised spirits of seekers for light. Contrast this with the condescension and the rejection so-called witnesses hurl at those in the bondage of some evil habit. Contrast this with the cold indifference to lives torn loose from their moorings, drifting into the oblivion of eternal damnation.

Jesus cared. Cared for those wandering in lostness. Cared for the sinner in his bondage. Cared for the sinner in his crushing despair. To save them from this and all the bitter fruit of sin He had come.

Jesus was a friend of sinners. Inherent in this friendship so freely offered was full acceptance. He had come into the world for this purpose—to redeem. To bring back to Himself. He had come precisely to accept them. To have rejected them would have been a denial of His purpose in coming to earth.

When Christians do not offer full acceptance to the sinner, they deny their part in Christ's redemptive work. They deny Christ. They witness to the fact that His love has not yet captured them and does not now control them.

Acceptance does not overlook sin. Sin must always be reckoned with. But sin is never cause to reject the sinner. The fact of the sin is the very reason Christ's love is reaching out, through us, to the sinner. The presence of sin does not provide an opportunity for petty little human judges to pass sentence upon the sinner for his actions. Acceptance means an extension of Christian warmth without any reservations based on the kind of lives individuals are living. We must take them as they are, unlike ourselves perhaps, unloving and unlovable, but persons for whom Christ died. The warmth of our accepting love must reach across our differences, past their reluctance, deeply into their need. It must dissolve the walls of prejudice: racial, national, academic, religious, denominational. It must crush the fancy structures of self-righteous pride in religious heritage and station. It must crumble the shale of intolerance separating men from men.

Perhaps the most acutely practical point of acceptance relates to the matter of participation with non-Christian friends in questionable activities. This is understandable. The Christian has determined the path of obedience down which his loyalty to Christ will take him. He willingly avoids certain habits or practices because they harm his body, hinder his testimony, hurt others, or simply because they are forbidden the child of God. He recognizes the lordship of Christ in all he does and will not knowingly dishonor his Master.

True acceptance of the non-Christian never needs to bring the rightness of this position into question.

The real problem lies not in an uncompromising loyalty to

Christ but rather in our lack of grace in refusal. Consequently we often embarrass, if not insult, those who offer the courtesy of a drink or a cigarette or who invite us to share in an activity against which we have convictions. Close acquaintance usually eliminates the problem, but sometimes initial refusals are given in such poor taste that close acquaintance becomes impossible.

The Christian need not feel apologetic when he draws the line at a certain point. It can be done graciously and with genuine appreciation for the thoughtfulness of the individual. He can say "no, thank you" to a cigarette with as much honesty and with as little judgment as he would to a chocolate bar. After all, the main point of testimony is never what the Christian dare not do. Rather, it is what Jesus Christ has come to mean in his life.

Deliberate judgmental behavior of any kind, whether in a spoken response, or distasteful grimace, or sanctimonious action, will usually be seen as a rejection. At that point, the Christian has cut himself off from the next step in the path to relationship. Perhaps the simplest rule to follow in such circumstances is to avoid any kind of response which will embarrass your friend publicly. If clearly necessary, and opportunity affords, a private explanation will usually suffice—and the witness has retained the right to continue his involvement.

Again and again, the dedicated witness will find himself stumbling over the point of acceptance. His prejudices are deeply buried and seldom has his heritage of Scriptural teaching differentiated between person and act. As a result, there will be a constant struggle when seeking to offer full acceptance to those whose lives are cluttered with baubles or soiled by vice. The only antidote to the poisonous attitude of rejection lies in remembering that the incarnation illustrated supremely God's acceptance of sinful man at the same time as He abhorred his sin. This lesson we too must learn. There is no better place than at the cross.

c. Dialogue. The point where dialogue can begin marks real progress. In fact, dialogue represents the first flowering of relationship. Acquaintance forms the bridge to, but hardly constitutes, relationship. And acceptance only opens the door. But dialogue moves actively and pointedly toward the uncovering of inner selves, in part, the essence of relationship.

Dialogue is to relationship what blood is to life. Without it, relationship is dead. Without it, individuals remain ignorant of each other, far apart, basically unconcerned. Without it, indifference blights the soul and chills the heart. Without it, community is unknown, friendship an impossibility, and fellowship only a word.

Without dialogue, witnessing is a farce!

If witnessing were sermonizing, then our one-sided monologues could qualify. Most Christians, if they speak at all, only speak; they do not stop long enough to listen. Or they have not considered listening to be significant. Or they have been so enamored of their own slick words, to listen would be an affront to their ability which must find expression.

Such see the listener only as an ear, without a mind to think, or a heart to feel, or a will with which to respond intelligently. An automaton who, when the right button is pushed, will automatically mouth the correct clichés, signifying that the job is done and the "witness" can look for another ear.

But the serious Christian witness recognizes that he has much to learn. He learns by allowing opportunity for reaction. He learns by listening and meditating. Indeed, he will never be certain how to make the Gospel completely relevant until he waits quietly long enough to hear the heartbeat of another life. When this comes through, the Spirit-given sensitivity in his own being will draw out of his experience those dramas which prove him human, "a man of like passion," and which illustrate the power of God.

In fact, the great function of dialogue is to share experiences, reactions, conclusions, problems, frustrations, joys, sorrows, pleasures, and pain. Dialogue, honestly entered into, increasingly opens up the hidden recesses of ideas and thoughts. The real persons begin to emerge. This is precisely what must happen before relationship can be firmly established.

For the Christian, unaccustomed to uncovering his real self,

except perhaps to his closest Christian intimate, this can be a difficult, even a fearful, experience. He will rationalize by insisting
that none else should need to carry his burdens, that all is well,
that no one else would understand, or that his wish to be counsel-
or will be undercut by honest confession. But in his sneaky mind
he knows that pride keeps him from sharing deeply what he is
really like.

He fails to realize that absolute honesty can be refreshing.
To admit he faces problems, encounters strong temptations, or
fails at times, takes him out of the "goody-goody, so righteous"
class and puts him back into the human race. It can provide
actual encouragement for the non-Christian to face himself and
then turn to the One whose grace makes possible a new perspective, a new strength, new life.

For this too is a part of the sharing. Problems, temptations,
and failure can come to the Christian. But he thrills to report the
evidence of solutions, victory, and forgiveness. The witness of
God's grace stands out in dynamic vibrancy because it meets
human need. The disciple of Christ, in sharing his pilgrimage
through the shadows, also provides the setting in which to tell
naturally of the sunlight now shining in his life.

For the non-Christian, such dialogue can be a revelation.
*Here is a man, like me, but with some answers. And finding
more. A fresh outlook on life. No guilt complex. Believes he has
forgiveness. Meaning and significance in what he does. Unusually
kind and understanding.*

So he goes on, probing his own experience, contrasting lostness with direction, despair with hope, unbelief with faith, fear
with confidence, hate with love, uncertainty with assurance. And
as he looks at himself, he cannot evade the silent question in the
contrasts. *Could this be for me as well?*

All this the Spirit of God can accomplish when the witness
has been faithful in dialogue.

Of course, dialogue always remains a part of relationship,
from its first tentative probings to the deep involvements which
may follow. From each side, witness or the giving of evidence is

going on—on the one hand, evidence of despair and lostness, and on the other hand, an answering echo, but with a note of hope; hope realized and confirmed in the daily walk with Christ.

d. Friendship. The interaction of dialogue paves the way for the mutuality of friendship. For friendship must be a mutual, two-way experience. Friendliness can be shown without response. Even love can flow out to another—inferior or enemy—without a return in kind. But friendship can exist only where there is some degree of assumed equality as well as reciprocity.

Fortunate is the Christian witness who has seen his relationships with non-Christians move to this level of mutual regard. Contrasted with the tensions of early acquaintance, the struggles toward acceptance, the energetic probing of dialogue, and certainly the intensities of later involvement, friendship is a quiescent state. Repose marks the relationship. This is a plateau free from anxiety, emotionalism, and agitation. Restful.

Of course, at least two conditions will have been met for this experience to become reality. In the first place, there has been full and mutual acceptance of each other. Differences are recognized but do not become barriers. A climate for dialogue continues, although the aggressive quality of early exchanges has given way to quiet sharing. The major issues have been defined; positions are clear. Now the give-and-take of conversation turns to the refinement of ideas and gentle testings of detail in viewpoint. The wariness is gone; in its place a warm glow of confidence and genuine affection wraps the friends together—dissimilar in certain respects, but individuals, each accepting fully the personhood of the other.

Secondly, and this is wrapped up in the first, the non-Christian friend will be seen as a person, not as an *object for evangelism*. Perhaps this represents the most treacherous point in the whole experience of relationship. Unless clarity prevails here, the redemptive influence of our lives and love can be overshadowed quickly and irrevocably by a subtle urgency to succumb to statistical motivations. A concern for numbers now devastates all our efforts to this point.

Friendship must be earned, deserved, and maintained without ulterior motive. As long as the non-Christian is seen as a person, no problem exists. But as soon as he becomes a number, our attitudes will change, imperceptibly at first but nonetheless certainly, and the carefully woven cord of love will unravel before our eyes.

A very subtle distinction should be emphasized here. Witnessing as an exercise to be engaged in may have as goal the salvation of a person. In this case, a so-called ulterior motive is present. However, when witness is seen as the by-product of the Christlike life, this need not be true, except as Christ's compassion for needy men permeates and controls all our actions. Then one may question whether motive exists at all separate from His love flowing through us. This will be discussed further in the following chapter.

At least, the one to whom we witness, our friend, dare not be looked upon as a potential statistic, a name to be added to the membership list, another milestone in the effort against communism, or an added color bar on our service uniform. He does not represent another notch to be nicked into the stock of our Gospel gun or another hapless scalp to be hung from our ecclesiastical belt. He is not the pawn in a game between good and evil, to be pushed from one side of an imaginary line to the other, thus justifying self-congratulation because our side is winning. He is not just a number in the mass, a nonentity—he is a person.

We must see him beloved of Christ, a man for whom Christ died. We must see him as an individual facing situations from which Jesus Christ can deliver him. We must see him as the friend he has become to us, the one for whom we pray for our friendship will become a key to abundant living.

The depersonalization of both the unsaved masses and the drunkard down the street is an insult to God the Creator and Redeemer. He made persons; in Christ He has come to save persons. The crude impersonality of certain witnessing approaches denies the individuality of man, is un-Christlike and unscriptural.

Even friendship and visitation evangelism, so-called, are

inherently dangerous. While developed and practiced, in many cases, with honesty and dedication, they have not escaped easily the trap of an ulterior motive. The real problem with organized activities is that they are organized. Seldom are they spontaneous with the participants. This results too often in a stiff formality, a job to be done and gone, another report for the record.

True friendship evangelism can never be fully organized. A man finds his friends where he will, not ordinarily where he is told to. His normal contacts provide the potential for friendship. But the flower of friendship cannot be forced. It blooms only when the root is planted in the proper soil and the sunshine and rain have come in abundance.

The church may help its members learn to be friends. Indeed, the nurture of Christians for the purpose of being redemptive should be the essential ministry of the church. It provides some of the resources; it offers opportunities to share experiences; it welcomes those who, warmed by the love of a believer, seek further light. But it can hardly superimpose a rigid formalized structure on that which, by its nature, is always spontaneous and individualistic.

Visitation evangelism is defended, by some, as the method used by Jesus as well as by the early church. Whether the pattern so named today had its counterpart in those days would be difficult to prove. At any rate, the reports we have of Jesus' methods as well as those of the apostles indicate a high regard for the person. This did not necessarily exclude ministries to groups or perhaps even a systematized approach. But the emphasis seems to have been personal.

Whatever the adjective given to evangelism, the temptation to categorization is always present. The limitations of a category ignore the totality of Christian experience and the continuity in witness and influence. For the Christian, no part of his life is exempt from the lordship of Christ. Consequently, no activity or word can escape contributing to the overall message given by his life. As a friend, as a visitor, as a fellow businessman, as a neighbor, if he is Christian, he will be a witness for Christ.

Friendship is a relationship of mutual regard, carefully built through acquaintance, acceptance, and dialogue. It is honest, unforced. A common desire to know the other person, as a person, marks the experience. The Christian will be a friend because this is the ministry to which Christ calls him. He will be a channel for the friendship and love of Christ. Whether the non-Christian friend ever comes along to church or makes an immediate outward profession will make no difference to the Christian. If it does, his friendship has been a pretense and hypocritical—less than friendship.

However, where true friendship exists, the Spirit of God has an excellent framework within which to work. His work is to exalt Jesus Christ. He does this through the lives of yielded Christians. Through the witness of lives changed and being changed by the grace of God, He gets a message across to searching hearts. In the final analysis, He is the evangelist. We constitute the message.

e. Identification. True friendship provides a base upon which rests the next step in relationship—identification. Of course, elements of identification may show up in acquaintance, become involved in acceptance, emerge in dialogue, and are definitely present in friendship. But there comes a point between friends where a serious relationship demands more than mutual regard; it demands identification.

To identify is "to assert or prove to be absolutely the same. To join with; unite."

Here is where the high cost of commitment to witness begins to appear. The early steps of relationship can be entered into quite easily. However, identification carries a price tag that forces careful consideration. And yet what it costs to identify actually becomes only the down payment when compared with the continuing cost of involvement and servanthood and suffering.

Identification moves in two directions. In the first place, it relates to Christ and His mission. "God so loved the world, that he gave his only begotten Son. . . ." Jesus came into the world to save sinners. He died to redeem men. Now His Spirit lives in the world to exalt Christ and to direct the body of Christ, the church, of which He is the Head. The Head of the body determines the actions of the body members. For members of the body have no objectives or purpose apart from the Head. In other words, they identify themselves with Him in the fulfillment of His mission.

Theoretically, Christians accept this without dispute. The practical expression of identification with Christ is another matter, however.

Identification with Christ requires participation; participation in His love, in His forgiveness, in His compassion, in His serving and healing and reconciling ministry, in His rejection and suffering, in His death. In short, to be fully identified with Christ is to share in all that His mission implied. Anything less than this is not identification and serves only to distort His image in the world and frustrate His mission to mankind.

The Christian witness stands before man in Christ's stead, fully identified with Him in His purpose and concerns.

To follow Christ in this way leads us, in the second place, to the lesson of the incarnation. In this act, Jesus Christ identified Himself fully with man. He took upon Himself flesh, and the burdens of a fleshly existence. He walked the path of human travail. Physical hunger, extreme weariness, and emotional sensitivities became His lot. Limitations of time and space pressed in upon His divinity. The aloneness of His mission dogged His footsteps. In coming to earth in the form of man, Jesus stepped into man's situation. He joined with man in his need. He identified with man.

To this, the Christian witness is also called. In fact, this is the very foundation upon which rests his mission to share.

First of all he acknowledges his own humanity, the similarity of his creaturely and human identity, his commonality with all men, his essential unity in need and frustrations and hopes. He admits his fleshliness.

But he goes even further than this in identification. He takes upon himself or absorbs the humanity of his non-Christian friend.

The crudities, the repulsive habits, the crass materialism, the tantrums, the envy and hatred. He confesses that all this reflection of humanness is but a picture of the latent corruption in his own heart. But identifying with it, he also illustrates how the grace of God can overcome the humanness of man and transform the human heart into something divinely attractive.

Identification with the non-Christian, we said, carries a price tag. Written on this price tag may be inconvenience, boredom, ridicule, misunderstanding from every quarter, uncertainty, the name of heretic and revolutionary, suffering, and death. However, this is the way of the witness. This is the real goal of incarnation, the Word made flesh. This is the way of the cross— ultimately the only instrument of redemption.

f. Involvement. Involvement is locked in step with identification. "To join with" man in his humanity brings a train of costly results. Involvement goes deeper than implication; it reflects close entanglement, an almost inextricable or inseparable joining or combining.

Of course, this situation is already foretold in identification. God identified Himself so completely with the needs of men that He took on their humanity. The incarnation represented the ultimate in "joining with." This act constituted a complete involvement of God with man, an entanglement that ended only in death. But it was precisely this entanglement and death which brought life. We now are "partakers of the divine nature" only because Jesus partook of human nature. Without His involvement in man's dilemma we could not experience release from that dilemma.

The path of involvement is hard; yet no other path contributes more to witness, illustrates better the sufficiency of grace, or presents more graphic evidence of God's love. He who would witness of Christ in the fullness of His mission cannot evade this road. To turn from it is to deny the message he seeks to give as well as the Christ he claims to follow.

The politics of heaven have never allowed an isolationist policy with respect to man. Ambassadors of that kingdom, by virtue of accepting their appointment, commit themselves to the same.

This many Christians have forgotten or ignored.

Correctness and orthodoxy often shun involvement with an individual. In fact, professing Christians, congregations, and denominations have shunned involvement so long, they have ended up on a plateau of utter irrelevance. They disdain the valleys filled with the wrenching bitterness of blasted hopes. They turn from the highways choked with the traffic in blighted souls. They run from the hideous cries of those lost in the night.

Perhaps it is well. For if they were there, they would shrink from the soiled hands clutching for help.

High in a perfumed religious fog, they see only each other. And they hear only faintly the distant clamor below. Their noses closed to the stench of sin and their cloaks tucked carefully about them, they pick their lily-white way to personal damnation.

This is not the church of Jesus Christ.

The church is found where the Master is found.

The religious leaders of Jesus' day paid Him a compliment by commenting on the company He kept. "And Levi [the publican—tax collector] made him a great feast in his own house: and there was a great company of publicans and of others that sat down with them. But their scribes and Pharisees murmured against his disciples, saying, Why do ye eat and drink with publicans and sinners? And Jesus answering said unto them, They that are whole need not a physician; but they that are sick. I came not to call the righteous, but sinners to repentance."

To Zacchaeus He said, "For the Son of man is come to seek and to save that which was lost" (Luke 19:10).

Jesus came into the world to save sinners. He came not to a distant part of the globe. He came to sinners, into their midst, confronting them with His holiness, surrounding them with His love, entwining and entangling Himself with them in their need. Utterly involved to the death—and out of this came life.

There seems to be much confusion, among Christians, between separation and isolation. Separation from the world should never be synonymous with isolation from the sinner. Separation from the world, in its positive form, is separation unto Christ—complete identification with Christ. And we cannot reach this level of life in Christ without following Him to a personal involvement with sinful persons in their need. Christ's mission has always been to love—His life in us reflects the same.

It is normal for the new Christian to experience a great transformation of interests and relationships with other people. This is as it should be. However, if this new experience of regeneration actually results in an isolation from those for whom he now has a message, then he has missed the point of his new life. The dynamic of new life in Christ never takes us away from need; on the contrary, it always plunges us deeply into involvement with need.

A key to witnessing, as it relates to involvement, is availability. Without this element, witnessing is but a superficial marginal effort and deep involvement is an impossibility. Availability costs time, parts of a life; it costs inclination, the desire to help; it costs effort, determined action to find the relevancy of the Gospel for the problems at hand.

Availability hinges partly on perceptiveness to need and the opportunities in certain situations. Sometimes God's opportunities for a special witness come disguised as interruptions in a planned routine. All of life as well as every encounter will be seen as a time to reflect the life of Christ. But the witness will seek to develop an acute sensitivity to those circumstances in a life where a unique touch of God's love can carry extra meaning.

Of course, this sensitivity is not contingent alone or even primarily upon personality traits or human ability. The Spirit of God functions here in the life of each Christian to reveal need. Then He also makes possible the right response to need.

One evening, following a church service, my wife and I met a young lady. At that time she was a rather casual acquaintance.

"How are you, Helen?" I asked.

"Quite well, thank you," she answered, looking straight at me.

With an insight that can be ascribed only to the Spirit, I saw several things in her answer and in her face. She was struggling to be honest in her response but was unwilling to remove entirely the polite veneer of correct response. I felt she was using "quite" not with its earlier meaning or as the British use it—very —but rather with a looser meaning as Americans many times use it—almost. I thought I detected a hunger in her eyes, a kind of need.

So I said, "Would you like to tell me about it?"

She looked at me a long moment, struggling in her heart with the answer she wanted to give but couldn't verbalize. Finally she whispered, "How did you know?"

There was only one answer. "God told me just now."

She nodded, "Could I talk to you sometime?"

Thus began a friendship which led our family into a deep involvement with desperate need, and I trust also into true servanthood.

The Holy Spirit had been faithful in providing insight and an impulse to respond accordingly. Thus He works to bring resource and need together.

Apart from the compulsion to involvement inherent in Christlikeness, the ultimate objective of involvement is relevancy. An irrelevant gospel is not gospel, for the Gospel is good news of deliverance. And a gospel that cannot function relevantly and redemptively in the midst of conflict and struggle and hatred and sin is not good news. In fact, it is bad news! To imply redemption and fail to fulfill the promise because of irrelevancy undercuts the mission of God in Christ, besmirches His name, and reflects a dishonesty utterly contradictory to the character of our Father.

Involvement to witness calls for soldiers, not spectators. The battle must be joined. The issue of our times must be faced. Our lives must be committed—committed to an entanglement with the burdens of humanity. Committed to show how Jesus helps man bear these burdens through relationship to God. Committed to expendability. Committed to those hearts filled with meaninglessness who must taste the tangy salt of His purpose in their lives. Committed to those blind eyes who grope through the darkness and call for a light—the light of His presence—the light we bear in our beings.

g. Servanthood. "For we preach not ourselves, but Christ Jesus the Lord; and *ourselves your servants for Jesus' sake*" (II Corinthians 4:5). "For though I be free from all men, yet have I made myself *servant unto all,* that I might gain the more" (I Corinthians 9:19).

Each step toward another person rubs the glamour off relationship and uncovers its hard reality. Of course, relationship carries its rewards as well. But the witness cannot ignore either the normal burden that human relationship implies or the special demands his own identification with Christ requires. The servanthood of Jesus Christ is reflected always in the relationship His followers sustain to others.

A witness to Jesus Christ—the evidence of His redemptive work in a life—and servanthood are inextricably linked together. The mark of a witness goes far beyond the glib recital of historical facts, the display of religious knowledge, or the quick pressure and condescension of a hurried invitation. The mark of a witness is identical to the badge of a servant—"ourselves your servants for Jesus' sake."

Service always tests commitment to a cause. Espousal of objective, agreement to a principle, shared theory are one matter. But a translation of philosophy into reality calls for a quality of belief not often found in a practical definition of faith. Servanthood tests dedication doubly: first in terms of honesty of purpose and intention and secondly in terms of the character of the reflection of Jesus' life in us.

The servanthood of believers is rooted in the concept of a serving God. His power and majesty sometimes overshadow this aspect of God's character. He is the Creator, Sustainer of life, Lord of the universe. But He also became the veritable Servant of man through Christ. His divinity and infinity make His servanthood the more impressive. His purity makes His involvement with sinful man a startling revelation of power. And His justice makes His love all the more of grace.

A servant people is no accident. To be servant is in the tradition of our Father. As God broke through into history, so His servant people involve themselves in the difficulties of men. They witness to the power of God through the incarnation of Christ's life in theirs, through the divine Word made literal flesh.

Jesus went everywhere serving people. Not in a so-called religious sense. Much of what He did would today be called social service. Yet, although His acts toward men bore no specific religious mark, in the traditional sense, everything He said and did bore the mark of His Father's love and concern. "No man hath seen God at any time; the only begotten Son, which is in the bosom of the Father, he hath declared him" (John 1:18). "And the Word was made flesh, and dwelt among us, (and we beheld his glory, the glory as of the only begotten of the Father,) full of grace and truth" (John 1:14).

This was God loving people, caring for people, serving people.

The witness, as servant, reflects supremely this essence of grace.

Service to the unsaved is never bait. It is given freely, with no strings attached or no response or reciprocity demanded. True love and servanthood demands no greater motivation than the Christ serving through us the need we see.

To use service as a lever to pry people into church attendance or membership denies the character of love. To serve with hope of merit or ecclesiastical gain contradicts the definition of grace. To serve, and yet not truly be servant, mocks our Servant-leader and empties our message of meaning. Thus our witness is invalidated.

The core of servanthood is self-giving. Not things, but self. Not cash, but time. Not one's marginal residue, but one's life.

The Christian witness invests a part of his own life in the spiritual welfare of another. He does not count the cost but gives himself freely—as did Christ who gave Himself so completely to the needs of men that the gift of Himself ended in His own death

Martin Luther caught this spirit when he said, "I will give myself to my neighbor as Christ gave Himself for me. I will take upon myself even the sins of my neighbor as Christ took my sin upon Himself." This involves the daily living of the Christian as well as his death to self.

Jesus gave Himself—in living and in dying. He redeemed man through His self-giving. His gift to the human race was not so much the miracles He performed, or the multitudes He fed, or the suffering He endured. All these were evidences of His giving. But the real gift was Himself—the gift of Himself to people. Since He was infinite and divine and perfect, He gave of Himself infinitely and completely and with full revelation of God's love.

Such giving is beyond us, humanly speaking. Yet as we are yielded to His Spirit and as we become extensions of His servant hood, He gives Himself through us. The extent of His servant hood is limited only by our commitment. Our self-giving reflect the point to which He has changed our lives. This is the incon trovertible evidence which constitutes our witness.

There are at least three kinds of giving which reflect servant hood and express witness: word gifts, deed gifts, and feeling gifts.

Word gifts are perhaps the easiest to give. This does not mean they are of less value or insincere. On the contrary, an appropriate word gift presented at the right time, wrapped in a voice tone touched with love, and beribboned with a gracious smile, can change an individual's day—or life. Concern, kindness and willing servanthood can be conveyed simply but profoundly through word gifts carefully chosen.

Deed gifts are more concrete than either of the other two. A cup of cold water, an extra step, an hour's work, a cheering visit—each one befits the servant role. And each one reflects a Christlike self-giving.

Feeling gifts, sometimes, are the most difficult to share. Sympathetic understanding without condescension, empathy, and full emotional involvement require a sensitivity that is nothing less than a gift from God. Few individuals possess this gift natur lly. However, the great Giver of gifts, if we will, can break our hearts to tune them with the broken hearts around us. Feeling gifts are often unspoken. Words become superfluous. Even deeds clatter noisily against the emptiness of one who needs a feeling gift. Just to be near, and knowing of the need, provides a strength no other gift can afford. This too is witness.

Of a university student it was said, ". . . the frontal attack of religious emphasis is as nothing in comparison with the effectiveness of ————————, whose principle 'elective' consists in belonging to other students for Christ's sake." He had learned to give himself away, a true servant, an incontrovertible witness.

Or a dying minister, following a serious and prolonged illness, even against the background of commitment to the will of God, said, "I wish I could go on living a while and just be the love of God to people." This is the ultimate in servanthood, the greatest gift—to be the love of God to people.

h. Suffering and death. To accept the finished character of Christ's sacrifice is theologically correct. But this represents only half the theology of redemption. Redemption continues and is still operative in the world today, insofar as the life and purposes of Christ are functional in His followers. Redemption was accomplished historically in one act. At the same time, redemption has become a continuum into and through the present. It is now represented in the body of Christ, the church.

The historical character of the cross of Christ tends to blind Christians to the relevance of the cross today. Gethsemane and Golgotha have been sentimentalized too easily and their reality for today overlooked. But there is little evidence to present to the non-Christian apart from this reality.

The cross has become a symbol, justifiably and unfortunately. Justifiably, because a symbol recalls from memory a basic truth. Unfortunately, because, as a symbol, it is devoid of the brutality, the blood, the pain, and the utter agony which accompanied its use.

We see the empty cross against a breaking sky and thrill to the truth of resurrection. But we forget that the cross represents not only an altar upon which was offered the perfect sacrifice and from which the broken body was taken to be laid in a tomb. The cross also represents a goal, an objective; in one sense, the end of the road, although in another sense only the beginning.

None would deny the suffering of Christ as He drew near to His death. Even in the midst of steadfast purpose, the cry from his physical being was for another way. The anguish in the garden uncovered His humanity in a marked manner and began to reflect the great price He was to pay so that men could know God. The nail-pierced hands and feet, the torn side, the agony of thirst, the torture of mockery, the terrifying despair of separation from God, can never be reproduced. And yet this suffering stands as a marker on the path the witness walks as he gives evidence of the miracle of God's grace.

There can be acquaintance without acceptance; acceptance without dialogue; and dialogue without friendship. But there cannot be honest identification with men in their need without involvement and servanthood and suffering.

To speak of these latter steps in relationship as an aspect in the methodology of witnessing sounds almost irreverent. Still, in the final analysis, there is no other method. Until relationship exists, the giving of evidence remains a churchly activity, an exercise to keep our religious muscles in trim. And when relationship does exist, there will be suffering.

To enter the lives of those with whom we relate opens the door to rejection, misunderstanding, the bearing of burdens, tears, and heartache. In this setting, either the grace of God reveals its potential, or the farcical character of our profession is uncovered. The rugged bumps of daily living and routine problems are absorbed through Christ or the bruises reflect to the world the thin veneer of our faith. Sharing honestly and fully places our shoulders under the sodden weight of frustration and meaninglessness and guilt. This can show the miraculous resource of strength from God. Or it highlights the stumbling collapse of human effort.

The heat of a life lived without God, applied to the crucible of shared suffering, becomes the test of grace. Sufficiency here constitutes the witness. And this is the essence of redemption.

On the following day, John saw Jesus coming toward him and said, "Look, there is the lamb of God who will take away the sin of the world! This is the man I meant when I said 'A man comes after me who is always in front of me, for he existed before I was born.' It is true I have not known him, yet it was to make him known to the people of Israel that I came and baptized people with water."

Then John gave this testimony: "I have seen the Spirit come down like a dove from Heaven and rest upon him. Indeed, it is true that I did not recognize him by myself, but he who sent me to baptize with water told me this: 'The one on whom you will see the Spirit coming down and resting is the man who baptizes with the Holy Spirit!' Now I have seen this happen and I declare publicly before you all that he is the Son of God!"

On the following day John was again standing with two of his disciples. He looked straight at Jesus as he walked along and said, "There is the lamb of God!" The two disciples heard what he said and followed Jesus. Then Jesus turned round and when he saw them following him, spoke to them. "What do you want?" he said.

"Master, where are you staying?" they replied.

"Come and see," returned Jesus.

So they went and saw where he was staying and remained with him the rest of that day. (It was then about four o'clock in the afternoon.) One of the two men who had heard what John

said and had followed Jesus was Andrew, Simon Peter's brother
He went straight off and found his own brother, Simon, and tol
him, "We have found the Messiah!" (meaning, of course, Christ
And he brought him to Jesus.

Jesus looked steadily at him and said: "You are Simon, th
son of John. From now on your name is Cephus" (that is, Peter
meaning "a rock").

The following day Jesus decided to go into Galilee. H
found Philip and said to him, "Follow me!" Philip was a ma
from Bethsaida, the town that Andrew and Peter came from
Now Philip found Nathanael and told him. "We have discovere
the man whom Moses wrote about in the Law and about whom
the Prophets wrote too. He is Jesus, the son of Joseph, and come
from Nazareth."

"Can anything good come out of Nazareth?" retorte
Nathanael.

"You come and see," replied Philip. (John 1:29-46, Phillips

5

OUR MOTIVATION

In chapter two we discussed a variety of factors which block or distort a Christian's witness. Among them were spiritual hindrances. One of these was the matter of improper motivation. Here, we should like to explore further the matter of motivation in witness.

Practically any physical activity presupposes motivating or stimulating force. Even in reflexive actions, there has probably been a certain stimulus provoking the response. The same is thought to be true in a spiritual sense. In other words, every religious exercise asks a "why?" What are the reasons for it? What are the motivations behind the action?

On the one hand, such frank questioning reflects a healthy desire for honest evaluation. On the other hand, however, it may represent a sidetracking preoccupation with reasons for action rather than action. And it could lead to an unfortunate misunderstanding regarding witnessing and the essential elements of forces which result in a witness being given.

As was true in the previous chapter, to discuss motivation in an analytical way is to risk a distortion of definition. Can an experience such as witnessing be dissected without destroying or at least twisting the understanding of its essence? Are there really motivating factors present in that which is inherently spontaneous? Is there such an experience as absolute spontaneity? May we not be doing violence to the ministry of the Spirit to confuse His work in us with a cold analysis of mechanistic activity —stimulus and response; objective and method; motivation and action? There are no easy answers to these questions.

Perhaps motivation is the wrong word. Past acquaintance with it and normal use tends to project an image of a psychological or almost mechanical process. Actually, our witness is inherent in our relationship to Jesus Christ. Apart from this relationship, there are no valid motivations. And when the relationship exists, its compelling influence can hardly be spoken of as motivation, although to some they may appear to be synonymous.

Any discussion of motivation to witness, therefore, must recognize the limitations just described. The word, at least because of association, does not adequately introduce or define the forces which result in witness. Yet there probably is none better. To talk of motivation with relation to witnessing is a little like attempting to define the motivation which takes us to the dinner table. A variety of elements combine to produce this motivation; but each is really secondary. Actually, our essential humanness is responsible. In something of the same way, the very fact that we are spiritually alive constitutes motivation to witness, if such it must be called.

Perhaps this can be enlarged upon. Physical aliveness places us in a sphere of activity where contact with others is normally unavoidable. Spiritual experience grants us the right to tell about it. Possession, by its own nature, obligates us to share. Need in others focuses our message, our actions, our service. Motivation, in one sense, therefore, is presence, experience, possession, and need all wrapped up in one package. Yet, in another sense, the word "motivation" almost demeans the true character of the spontaneous welling forth of Christ's life.

Stated in still another way, there can never be more than a single primary motivating factor present in the Christian witness,

although it is twofold in nature. The first aspect is simply my
new life in Christ (or Christ's life in me) And the second is that
life reaching out to men in need. It is simply that life living itself
out, reflecting its true nature. Resource and need, as separate
from each other as the far reaches of infinity, still are tightly
integrated into a single propellant into service. Like the chemical
and mechanical factors present in the phenomenon of internal
combustion, resource and need become one in their compulsive
force. As different as are the divine and the natural, their juxta-
position or being brought together provokes a response of witness
and service in the Christian. Call it motivation, if you will, but
note well its inextricable involvement with the life of Christ in
us, on the one hand, and the environment in which this life is
lived, on the other.

Having established, then, the essential compulsion to witness
—a compulsion born of the experience of grace, the new relationship with Christ, and an awareness of human need—we may move
on to recognize other factors, significant but secondary, which
support and confirm the basic motivation to witness. This first
and primary motivation is present, in a sense, in spite of ourselves.
That is, the resource has become ours through grace; the motivation is inherent in our spiritual existence. And the need of men
is present whether it calls forth a response or not; it exists as an
element in motivation only in the presence of Christ's outgoing
love.

However, the secondary motivations call for a response on
our part—a response of understanding, commitment, and action.
The extent and intensity of this response in turn enlarges our
hearts as channels for the resources to flow toward need. And it
increases sensitivity to the need which in its turn calls forth more
of God's love.

For this reason the so-called secondary motivations are not
insignificant. Indeed, they fulfill the requirement for volitional
and specific involvement in Christ's mission. In their place, they
fill an important role. But they dare not be confused with, nor
may they replace, the essential primary compulsion inherent in

the life of Christ facing and responding, through us, to the needs of men.

The volitional quality must always be present in Christian living. The Christian is not an automaton without the power for thought or personal action. From the first decision the will continues to be involved. This very fact makes possible the presence and control of Christ's Spirit which provides the essential compulsion to redemptive living. And it also provides the foundations on which are built the secondary motivations which underlie our commitment and energize our service.

1. *The motivation of honor.* The humble Christian never escapes the consciousness of his complete dependence on God for every blessing he enjoys. Some of these we shall discuss in greater detail. Suffice it to say here, however, that every creature apart from God is a spiritual pauper, destitute and doomed to an eternal, infinite poverty. Into this black gloom of wretched need reached a hand to lift man into the glories of fellowship with the Maker.

Only meditation can uncover the stark contrast between the "before" and "after." Even then, finite mind can barely grasp the reach of love that drew us into His presence, gave us His nature, and wrapped us around with the cloak of His righteousness. When snatches of comprehension are given, the child of God must join the psalmist in his grateful song, "I will praise thee, O Lord my God, with all my heart: and I will glorify thy name for evermore" (86:12). Or echo the words of the twenty-four elders who fall down before the all-glorious One crying, "Thou art worthy, O Lord, to receive glory and honour and power: for thou hast created all things, and for thy pleasure they are and were created" (Revelation 4:11). And sing with the vast host of angels, ". . . ten thousand times ten thousand, and thousands of thousands . . . Worthy is the Lamb that was slain to receive power, and riches, and wisdom, and strength, and honour, and glory, and blessing" (Revelation 5:11, 12).

To be conscious of who God is and what He has done for us, is to have born in our hearts a consuming desire to honor His name. To bring to His name glory, the exalted reputation it deserves.

Obviously, reporting our conclusions regarding the greatness of God constitutes a witness. Building up the reputation of God before others, honoring His name by telling about our experience with Him, sharing information about His character—all of this is at the heart of our message. In fact, to glorify Christ (to enhance His reputation) is the work of the Holy Spirit. The Spirit in us exalts Christ through every aspect of our lives.

This desire to honor and glorify the name of Christ is, in itself, a motivating factor. It permeates our consciousness; it infects every other motivation; it provokes our message and forms its content; it pervades our entire relationship with God.

"For His name's sake" controls the Christian's life. Apart from the compulsion inherent in the new life itself, to bring glory to His name becomes our strongest motivation.

2. *The motivation of grace.* Closely allied with the preceding is "our measure" of God's grace. For this constitutes the soil and the seed from which springs forth the desire to honor the name of Christ. They are barely to be separated, yet the marvel in both compels a careful look at each as a motive force.

Perhaps nothing surpasses the wonder of grace—favor undeserved. The human state is stranger to this quality of giving. For this reason, the grace of God seems to defy comprehension; at best we can claim but momentary and partial insight into the fullness of grace.

Simply stated, grace is the free and unearned quality of the Father's love. It is not separate from love and mercy; rather, an aspect of each. Grace defines more precisely the character of love. It reflects love's fullness; it illustrates the reach of love.

To be in grace is to enjoy the state of reconciliation with God through Jesus Christ. Fellowship with the Father, not as those receiving their right, but a gift—unearned and unearnable. Relationship, not of the law, but as a favor to the undeserving. Life, life in the Spirit, and in its train forgiveness, cleansing, peace—not of works, lest any should boast, but grace.

Grace is the wealth of heaven poured out into the empty heart of the pauper. Grace is the pardon of the cross granted to a criminal thrice condemned. Grace is the lifting of sin's burden crushing the spirit into hopeless despair. Grace is God's love given without charge.

In the face of all this, to speak of motivation seems almost superfluous. The simple awareness of grace should be a spark which ignites the spirit, propelling it into witness, driving the soul to share, in some sense reflecting grace itself to others undeserving. To acknowledge grace is to share it. To admit its work in one's life is to find a compelling motivation to witness.

3. *The motivation of miracle.* To see a miracle performed is a sight never to be forgotten. To watch the miracle in one's own life defies description.

No other word describes so well the result wrought by grace. At every point the increasing contrast between the past and the present, the old and the new, is so marked that only a miracle can account for the change. Note the following contrasts and measure the miracle they illustrate.

From a state of enmity with and separation from God man moves into the experience of reconciliation and consequent fellowship.

At one time we were aliens and strangers; now in Christ Jesus we have become fellow citizens with the saints, and of the household of God.

Children of disobedience, wayward and willful, are now children of light, having received adoption as sons.

Formerly dead in trespasses and sins, unmindful of right, insensitive to the Spirit, the new man is alive unto God.

Once filled with all unrighteousness, we find ourselves cleansed from all unrighteousness.

Before the great change in our lives we were without hope in the world. Since coming to Christ we are "looking for that blessed hope, and the glorious appearing of the great God and our Saviour Jesus Christ."

Whereas in the ignorance of sin and the blindness of unbelief we groped about without understanding, now is Christ Jesus "made unto us wisdom. . . ."

Ungodliness marks the character and life of a sinner. But in Jesus Christ, godliness or godlikeness becomes possible. Paul speaks of "the life . . . of Jesus . . . [being] made manifest in our body."

Undone, helpless, inadequate creatures—complete in Him in whom dwells all the fullness of the Godhead bodily.

Bitterness, anger, wrath, and malice have given way to kindness, a tenderhearted spirit, forgiving one another.

Where there was inescapable guilt, "there is therefore now no condemnation."

Where fear and uncertainty shook the soul, there has come a quiet confidence and trust.

Where turmoil once roiled the heart ("the wicked are like the troubled sea, when it cannot rest"—Isaiah 57:20), there is peace.

Those who were "by nature the children of wrath" have become "partakers of the divine nature."

And those who once "walked according to the course of this world, according to the prince of the power of the air" now "are led by the Spirit of God."

And thus are the sons of God.

This is the miracle of redemption!

As John of the epistles would say, "Behold!" Stop and gaze a while at this awesome spectacle, this miracle happening before your eyes, this miracle taking place even now in your heart. Every day in the family of God, each new reflection of Christlikeness constitutes a miracle.

Need one search further for motivation? Christ, the miracle worker, waits to walk with us to those maimed in body; to those halting in step; to those on the paralytic's bed; to those blind and dumb and deaf. The miracle of His life and likeness growing still within us propels us into witness.

4. *The motivation of hope.* "Hope maketh not ashamed." Hope, the right kind of hope, never leaves us embarrassed. Hope

centered in God carries a divine guarantee. Embedded in the Christian's hope is the seed of fulfillment, the right of expectation.

The Christian's hope revolves around two bright stars in the constellation of promise. The one star is the resurrection of Jesus from the dead. Shining just as brightly is His covenant to return.

Never is the night so long or the sky so dark but that these stars guide the child of God with certain ray, pointing always to a faith that finds reality in Christ whose resurrection validates the hope of His return.

Paul pinpoints the chill alternative to hope for the future. "If in this life only we have hope in Christ, we are of all men most miserable." To have a hope stopped by the grave is to have no hope at all.

But "He is not here . . . he is risen," still echoes in the chambers of time. However, it is more than a cry, more than a sudden revelation, more than a startling report. These words, harbinger of hope, constitute our message. From the time this announcement passed from angel lips and flitted from disciple to disciple, the news has spread. To those quickened and to those still dead in sin this glad cry vibrates across the cords of consciousness. To the latter an answering tug brings glorious life. With the former, the cry in concert crescendoes in waves of sound around the world, binding in glad fellowship those of kindred faith and pushing them out to share their hope—the only hope that man can have.

5. *The motivation of example.* Christ's journey from glory to humanity, from heavenly riches to abject poverty, from eternity into time, encompassed an incomparable span, bridged an immeasurable gap. To enshroud divine spirit in human flesh must have demanded a supreme motivation. And it did. Infinite love provides the only explanation.

Power could have found a thousand other ways to prove itself. Worship and praise might have been sung for ten thousand other more lofty reasons. Majesty and honor would seem to have dictated almost any other course of action than one of absolute humility. Even God's character could have been proclaimed without the involvement of incarnation, and was, through the Old Testament prophets.

But God chose to provide for love the infinite definition. So He took on Himself the creatureliness of His creation. No other testimony of His mercy and grace could have been spoken with greater eloquence than when "the Word was made flesh, and dwelt among us." This was an unmistakable proclamation, a statement of concern other than which there could have been no greater. "Have this mind among yourselves, which you have in Christ Jesus, who, though he was in the form of God, did not count equality with God a thing to be grasped, but emptied himself, taking the form of a servant, being born in the likeness of men. And being found in human form he humbled himself and became obedient unto death, even death on a cross" (Philippians 2:5-8, RSV).

"For ye know the grace of our Lord Jesus Christ, that, though he was rich, yet for your sakes he became poor, that ye through his poverty might be rich" (II Corinthians 8:9).

The downward steps of Christ's descent to humility provided for man the stairway to glory. His poverty opened the door to infinite riches. In this, Christ provided an example. And He also shows the way each of us must serve if we would follow Him.

Wherever commitment has bound a man to Christ, His example becomes a motivation for service and witness. But the love of Christ is far more than an example to provide motive. Christ's love actually moves the Christian rather than simply offering motivation. That is to say, the example itself becomes the resource. This may be a fine distinction, yet it is one that should be made, and that precisely.

Paul wrote, "the love of Christ constraineth us." Another version uses the word "control." Christ's love controls. It is His love in the Christian which flows out to need. And this is far different from our response to need because we love Christ.

Both are valid but different. Our love for Christ and our desire to follow His example of love may well establish a motivation which moves us to service. However, Christ's love controlling us goes supremely beyond any motivated action. It is literally Christ living His life in us and loving other people through us. His example then does provide motivation but more, much more. The example of Christ reveals the way He lives and loves today, in and through His children. It defines the actions and speech of Christians.

Perhaps the greatest lesson taught by the example of Christ is the non-motivational character of divine love. God loves, not because He is motivated by certain external circumstances but because He is love. His character is love. Therefore any expression of Himself reflects this essential characteristic of God.

The motivation value, then, of Christ's example lies only secondarily in the considered response of obedience it provokes. Primarily, the motivation to commitment and yieldedness issuing forth in His loving through us moves beyond stimulus and response and partakes of the essence of His life which is the supreme compulsion and inherent in our very spiritual existence.

6. *The motivation of concern.* Christlikeness implies compassionate concern. "Not willing that any should perish," Christ came to men, to live for them and die for them. All of His ministry reflected this concern—the time He took with people, the gentle word, the healing touch. And He walked the path of sacrifice, to the death, because compassion drew Him on.

In one sense, concern for the individual is also inherent in the new life Christ gives us, a facet of His love. In another sense, however, concern calls for an initial and a continuing response from us.

Much in our world dulls sensitivity and clouds our perception of personal needs. The secular atmosphere seems to stifle the spiritual dimension. Materialism distorts the measure of things in contrast to matters of the soul. The rush of schedule blinds us to the difference between the urgent and the important. Superficial contacts with people help us evade involvement and lead to indifference.

Concern demands attention and effort, energetic effort. This calls for a recognition of the barriers to concern as well as a deliberate decision to maintain sensitivity through a close walk with Christ *and* exposure to need. Without these factors there can be little or no concern. When they are present, concern grows and moves one increasingly into situations where witness takes place.

7. *The motivation of potential.* Not what I may become but what my friend may become through Jesus Christ. This may well be a deliberate intellectual, as well as spiritual, exercise.

Every human being carries within him certain seeds of potential development. They may be dormant throughout life because of ignorance, inertia, unfavorable circumstances, or tragedy. Or one or more may be discovered and nurtured until they flower into a thing of beauty and usefulness.

The same is true in the spiritual realm. By creation man belongs to God. But His image has been distorted, well-nigh destroyed, through sin. Christ's sacrifice has made possible a re-creation of God's likeness and a restoration of relationship. Every man now, sinner though he be, is potentially a child of God.

The Christian witness recognizes this potential in every one he meets. A new son of God, free from guilt, with peace in the heart and useful in service, becomes the picture the Christian sees as he looks at the sinner. Not what he is but what he can become in Christ. He supports this vision by recalling his own lostness and the discovery of himself. He confirms the possibility as he looks at the fellowship of believers and sees there the amazing transformations.

This knowledge of potential status and worth spurs the witness to faithful discipleship and witness.

But there is yet an added dimension. The spiritual potential in every man does not stand by itself. The Spirit of God at work in a life brightens personality, enhances natural abilities, often uncovers new talents, and certainly energizes the whole for the glory of God. In fact, one may question whether the average individual really knows himself and his capabilities. Such knowledge comes often to the Spirit-led person, newly sensitive and bold to step out in faith, testing the promises of God.

Man's potential, natural and spiritual, becomes a goad, then, to witness. I see not the pathetic picture of meaninglessness and moral disarray; but rather the vision of what that man may become as he yields himself to Jesus Christ. So I share myself freely in order to uncover this potential, knowing full well the release and joy this can bring.

8. *The motivation of urgency.* Perhaps the note of urgency needs less attention than the other points mentioned. For this tune has been sung far and wide with consequent distortion and much misunderstanding among Christians. Unfortunately also, in some circles, the urgency of the Gospel message itself has been ignored completely simply because valid reasons for urgency have grown out of balance with respect to other logical motivations.

Among the traditional reasons for urgency in witness are the fires of hell, the uncertainty of life, and the world crises. Others could be mentioned, but these suffice to characterize the problem. Of course, these are logical bases on which to found a philosophy of urgency. No conservative Biblical scholar denies the fact of eternal judgment upon sinners. All of us are aware of the brevity of time and the uncertainty of life. And not even the casual observer of the world scene can ignore the national and international shock waves winging around the globe from crisis after crisis. That any one of a number of these could erupt into catastrophe is beyond doubt.

So one develops a valid sense of urgency with a resultant motivation to energetic service. However, by themselves, these reasons for urgency, though they are Scriptural or obvious or both, bypass the more basic reasons and consequently a steadier motivation. And they sometimes completely overshadow more fundamental motivations.

Again, we must come back to the essential compulsive force in the Christian's life—the resources of Christ amidst human need. In one sense, taking into account degree, every need calls for action, with a certain measure of urgency built into the need. Were not some urgency inherent, one could question the validity of the need.

In its starkest application, there is no need of man so desperate as his spiritual need. To carry a crushing load of guilt, to search endlessly for personal significance and meaning in life, to be at enmity with one's fellow, to whip the senses in a vain effort to find a lasting joy—all this speaks a gnawing need crying for a satisfying answer. Where else should one look for a sense of urgency?

Or count the resources available in Christ. Measure the immeasurable! Stand at the storehouse door overflowing with grace waiting to be channeled to need. Any attitude less than urgency would proclaim a stinking selfishness, utterly unworthy of the profession we make. And an utter contradiction of the very nature of the Resource.

Behold the incarnation. God made flesh! This foray into creatureliness was not a weekend picnic. It was the urgent expression of character. The ultimate desperation of man called forth infinite love. Resource and need, as separate as divinity and humanity, came together in a white heat of divine compulsion, melted into one driving redemptive act.

Face the cross! Look upon the sacrifice Jesus offered—Himself. Who can deny the urgency inherent in the character of the gift or its object? The cross shouts urgency. It was not a Sunday afternoon relaxing device. The cross was an instrument of torture and death. Jesus struggled in His soul to avoid this agony. But the urgency of His mission drove Him to it.

In the face of this, to speak of the elements contributing to urgency usually considered is almost to miss the point. Of course, these elements are not to be ignored. But there is a single motivation to urgency, no, a compulsion, which extends the redemption of the cross into present need. The Christian who stands in the pathway of God's love to man does not need to ask for a sense of urgency and the push of motivation. He cannot escape being caught up in the flow of resource being poured out into need.

9. *The motivation of reproduction.* Whether powers of reproduction should be spoken of with relation to motivation could be debated. On the one hand, reproduction is seen as a

law of life, beyond dispute in any species. To speak of decision to reproduce probably is limited to the human race where experience and science have found ways to inhibit it. But normally, reproduction is the spontaneous result of physical principles.

On the other hand, in the spiritual realm, one must recognize that certain factors must be present for reproduction in kind to take place. Insofar as these factors rest within the power of the individual to choose may the motivation to reproduce be discussed. However, the spontaneous character of reproduction dare not be ignored; if it is, the effort of the flesh to bring to birth a spiritual being will be all too evident.

Three factors, then, should be noted. In the first place, powers of reproduction are normally inherent in life and its ordinary processes. Secondly, a healthy individual in the exercise of all his powers can no more abstain from reproducing himself (in God-ordained ways) than he can keep from breathing. Furthermore, similar laws of reproduction apply to the realm of the spiritual.

In other words, the normal Christian will be continuously involved in reproduction of the species. He may not often be aware when conception actually takes place. But he will certainly experience the joy of parenthood, at times fully conscious of his part in the new birth of an individual.

In this context, the motivation of reproduction sounds absurd. However, it must be remembered that reproductive powers demand spiritual health. It is at this point where the fruit of motivation becomes evident. Thus it is not so much a matter of motivation to reproduce, although this is recognized as a normal and a desirable end. Rather, the motivation to commitment takes precedence; so the life of Christ is truly seen and reproduction will be the result.

10. *The motivation of vocation.* In vocation lies a fundamental imperative that defies evasion. However, it is precisely at this point that many Christians attempt to excuse themselves from the responsibility of witnessing. Some may plead simple ignorance; many more may need to admit subscribing deliberately

to a distortion of vocation that allows a majority of Christians a degree of comfort in disobedience.

The Apostle Paul sensed an obligation not predicated on desire or personal wish. "For if I preach the gospel, that gives me no ground for boasting. For necessity is laid upon me. Woe to me if I do not preach the gospel! For if I do this of my own will, I have a reward; but if not of my own will, I am entrusted with a commission" (I Corinthians 9:16, 17, RSV).

"Entrusted with a commission" leaves no room for participation or disengagement at will. The fulfillment of a commission is not optional; it carries with it the pressure of responsibility.

The option is exercised at the point of decision to follow Christ. To respond negatively is to retain control of the will and the course of one's life. But to accept His call to discipleship fulfills the option and places one under His control. The new life in Christ becomes in essence a calling, a vocation, a consuming interest, a mission, a stewardship. There is no escape. To ignore this aspect of discipleship is to deny its essential nature.

What may be the sincere seeker's question. *How* reflects a simple and necessary humility. But *whether* is not in the disciple's vocabulary. The *whether* has been dealt with.

The call to vocation is as old as Abram. "Now the Lord . . . said unto Abram, Get thee out of thy country, and from thy kindred and from thy father's house, unto a land that I will shew thee . . . and thou shalt be a blessing . . . and in thee shall all families of the earth be blessed" (Genesis 12:1-3).

The call to vocation was confirmed by Christ. Jesus said, ". . . All power is given unto me in heaven and in earth. Go ye therefore, and teach all nations, baptizing them in the name of the Father, and of the Son, and of the Holy Ghost: teaching them to observe all things whatsoever I have commanded you: and, lo, I am with you alway, even unto the end of the world. Amen" (Matthew 28:18-20).

The call to vocation is as new as the newest follower. "And Jesus said unto them, Come ye after me, and I will make you to become fishers of men" (Mark 1:17).

Where response has been given, there is mission, commission, vocation, stewardship.

The motivation of vocation, therefore, comes from the understanding of what it involves. To be His disciple implies a new calling, participation in His redemptive work in the world. Awareness of this propels us into service.

Motivation is only a word until we see its fruit—a faithful proclamation of the living Word spoken by lip and life. From this beginning, born in faith and nurtured by the Spirit of God, a new creature is formed, a relationship is restored, a reconciliation is effected. As Christ is given control, His love is personified. This love, in turn, reflects God's grace and becomes a witness, a new proclamation of the living Word. Thus the cycle goes on, and on—with motivation immersed in His life in us.

The Christian is called to follow a good-neighbor policy—

At that moment Jesus himself was inspired with joy, and exclaimed:

"O Father, Lord of Heaven and earth, I thank you for hiding these things from the clever and intelligent and for showing them to mere children! Yes, I thank you, Father, that this was your will." Then he went on:

"Everything has been put in my hands by my Father; and nobody knows who the Son really is except the Father. Nobody knows who the Father really is except the Son—and the man to whom the Son chooses to reveal him!"

Then he turned to his disciples and said to them quietly:

"How fortunate you are to see what you are seeing! I tell you that many prophets and kings have wanted to see what you are seeing but they never saw it, and to hear what you are hearing but they never heard it."

Then one of the experts in the Law stood up to test him and said,

"Master, what must I do to be sure of eternal life?"

"What does the Law say and what has your reading taught you?" said Jesus.

"The Law says, 'Thou shalt love the Lord thy God with all thy heart and with all thy soul and with all thy strength and with all thy mind—and thy neighbor as thyself,' " he replied.

"Quite right," said Jesus. "Do that and you will live."

But the man, wanting to justify himself, continued,

"But who is my 'neighbor'?"

And Jesus gave him the following reply:

"A man was once on his way down from Jerusalem to Jericho. He fell into the hands of bandits who stripped off his clothes, beat him up, and left him half dead. It so happened that a priest was going down that road, and when he saw him he passed by on the other side. A Levite also came on the scene, and when he saw him he too passed by on the other side. But then a Samaritan traveler came along to the place where the man was lying, and at the sight of him he was touched with pity. He went across to him and bandaged his wounds, pouring on oil and wine. Then he put him on his own mule, brought him to an inn and did what he could for him. Next day he took out two silver coins and gave them to the innkeeper with the words: 'Look after him, will you? I will pay you back whatever more you spend, when I come through here on my return.' Which of these three seems to you to have been a neighbor to the bandits' victim?"

"The man who gave him practical sympathy," he replied.

"Then you go and give the same," returned Jesus. (Luke 10:21-37, Phillips)

6

OUR MISSION

Mission is an interesting word. Both root and modern use refer to a sending with a specific purpose. This is its basic Christian meaning as well. Later we shall look at its unfortunate misuse with consequent misunderstanding of *our mission*.

The Christian life and mission are bound together. Discipleship reflects mission. Our mission, in fact, is inherent in our relationship to Jesus Christ. Literally, we share in His mission by sharing His grace.

Witness and mission are part and parcel of each other. One cannot discuss message or method or motivation, with relation to witnessing, without discussing mission. Mission is woven into message. Method breathes mission. Motivation and mission are practically synonymous.

Yet, to see mission only as an element permeating the whole may be to overlook some essential truths. So in this chapter we shall attempt to explore a part of mission—that specifically related to objective as well as our own involvement in reaching that objective. In other words, where does mission take us? Does mission really involve me? To whom are we being sent? With what kind of person do we share?

1. *"Into all the world."* Usually, this brief quotation leads to discussion of the word *all*. That this is important, none can deny. However, for our purposes here, let us simply assume the universality of our mission: the Gospel should be preached in every land. From this point, then, we can go on to look, very briefly, at *the world*. What kind of world is this into which our mission takes us?

To some, this section will appear to be redundant. For news media of various kinds—television, radio, newspapers, magazines—carry a constant, almost overwhelming impression of our world. For others, a quick survey may add to an understanding of the world in which we live; the world into which Christ sends us.

It is a strange and wonderful world. An exciting world. A rapidly changing world. A world of hidden secrets. And a world of fascinating discoveries.

This world touches us who are experiencing God's grace and power. It affects our lives. It constitutes a danger and a challenge, a limitation and an opportunity. Understanding it, at least in part, shapes the content and form of our response to people living in it. When this is not true, witness can become pathetically irrelevant.

The world touches our neighbor also in many ways, some with more directness or intensity than others. It exerts an influence on him for both good and ill. It helps to make him what he is. It brings him certain advantages. It also produces certain kinds of needs.

The good news of salvation or redemption is divinely apropos to the needy person living in this kind of world. It is not too much to say, nor irreverent, that the Gospel was designed for people in this situation. Or, in other words, Jesus came upon the world scene precisely to provide answers for life here, as well as hereafter. Thrillingly, we are involved in God's redemptive work, in His reaching out to men. And yet in another sense, we are spectators, observing and marveling at the flow of His love and grace at work in us and others.

Into what kind of world has God's grace come? Where is the

arena in which resource meets needs? Against what backdrop is played the drama of grace on the stage of life? Let us look briefly at a few of the significant elements in today's world.

a. Our world is faced with fantastic population increases. By 1950 world population had reached 2,500,000,000. By the year 1964 another 500,000,000 had been added. By the year 2000 conservative estimates promise a total of five billion human souls. No country is immune from new and tremendous problems in the areas of food, space, housing, education, standards of living, politics, to name only a few, caused by this eruption of population.

b. Our world has become a shrinking neighborhood. No longer is it possible to ignore what transpires in Bangkok or Leopoldville or Brasilia or Tokyo. Advances in communication have made China a daily concern. They have brought South Africa to our front yard and Europe to the door. They have brought, via Tel-star, the pageantry of Rome and the drama of Alpine slopes into our living rooms. And world travel opportunities can change perspective in a matter of hours. Like it or not, few can escape some degree of emotional involvement with world problems.

c. Social disorganization characterizes much of the world today. Internationally, old alliances are broken almost casually and new ones formed; protectorates and colonies are erupting into self-determination; other countries, long dormant, are assuming new roles in world politics. Within many of these nations turmoil is the only word that can describe the changing scene— old patterns are suddenly broken down; racial entities are demanding and finding new relationships to each other; tribal populations, long desegregated within tight enclosures of separate culture, are being thrown together into the melting pot of new nationhood. Political communities, even in North America, have not escaped the blight of social disorganization—deterioration of the inner city, flight to the suburbs, the urbanization of rural areas, affluence and depression, racial conflict. Change is forced on whole neighborhoods within short years or even months. Orderly transitions, from decade to decade or generation to generation or century to century, can no longer be made. The result in many places is a rushing chaotic disorganization.

d. Scientific and technological advances have changed the world in which man lives as well as his attitude toward himself. He has proved himself an intrepid explorer, tenacious in his efforts to unlock the secrets of the universe. His mind ranges in interest from nuclear fission to electronic cooking. Physically, he pushes himself into the fringes of space. Seeming impossibilities are looked at only as challenges. Failures are seen in the light of their instructive value. He has turned his irrepressible curiosity to his scientific and technological advantage. With all of this, man begins to see himself as the center and sum total of the universe. He acknowledges no power higher than his own potential. The cult of the scientific and the technological has become a religion. Man's ability is supreme. Above this power there is no other.

e. Secularism follows closely on the heels of the above. Secularism—regard for worldly as opposed to spiritual matters—has become another religion, a system of faith and worship. It commands the commitment and loyalty of the masses. The pursuit of the secular has become a way of life. There is little antagonism to spiritual matters; they are simply ignored. Sometimes certain nonmaterial needs are recognized, but these are presumed to call only for an application of psychological resources. Much more often a deeper immersion in the material world is sought as the answer.

f. Depersonalization is one of the results of secularism. Persons matter little except as devices to reach material objectives. Of course, there are many other contributing factors as well—attitude toward time, the tempo of modern living, government procedures, manufacturing methods, merchandising developments, concentrations of population, housing arrangements, communications media. All of these and others have contributed to a mass approach with a resultant net loss of personal contact and the de-emphasis of personhood.

Men and women are social security numbers: digits, stick

figures, faces in hazy outline. They are a political mass to be manipulated. They are a market to be exploited: bodies to be clothed, stomachs to be fed. They are a housing development to be managed. They are an employee group to be used. They are a classroom to be taught. They are an audience to be preached to. But seldom are they individuals—persons with individual characteristics, special needs, private hopes and aspirations. Our world has taken the *person* out of *persons*. The result is a zero— and the slight hiss of meaninglessness.

g. Moral disintegration infects large areas of today's world. The climate of questioning search is not necessarily new, but the permissiveness which has followed the futile modern search for a standard seems to bear the stamp of the twentieth century. Systems of personal ethics which have stood for centuries have dissolved in a new climate of personal freedom. Moralities, long considered basic and germane to the structure of society, have suddenly withered away under the white heat of license. Even religious loyalties, many times a moderating influence, have shriveled into shrunken knots of memory, rattling along as useless baggage. In the world of today every man does that which is right in his own eyes.

h. Increasing amounts of leisure time mark large segments of the western world's population. The seven- and eight-hour day, the short workweek, and longer vacations open up great blocks of new leisure. This is both blessing and curse. Blessing because some of the pressures of past years have been relieved. Curse because the gift comes too often to those who have not yet learned to live with themselves. More time available only serves to emphasize their problems and complicate their search for meaning in life.

i. An atmosphere of uncertainty and lostness pervades much of the world today. Not the least responsible for this atmosphere of uncertainty is the centrality of a materialistic philosophy. When a more spiritual (i.e., less dependent on material or external evidence) philosophy guides a society, outward change has comparatively less effect on social stability and emotional equilibrium. However, when tangibles like money and houses and goods provide a foundation for faith and confidence, any major economic fluctuation or other catastrophe can be devastating. Moreover, the realities of personal problems or tragedy inevitably uncover the utter inadequacy of things as an anchor.

j. Irrelevant religion is also a part of the world in which we live. Great churches are built and lavish programs are carried out. Yet sadly, a Christian witness of concerned involvement too often is absent. Eyes are closed against the intrusion of desperate human need which could mar the quiet comfort of the weekly ritual. Passing by on the other side avoids the soiling contact that response to need seems to imply. Along with this, our world includes the fact of resurgent world religions, some of them remarkably attractive to harried moderns.

This is the world into which our mission takes us. A world of discovery. A world of change and uncertainty. A world of depersonalization. A world of moral disintegration. A world in which things have become god. A world of lostness and searching.

"Into all the world" sends the Christian witness to people upon whose lives this world is pressing its imprint. Every factor briefly mentioned, along with a host of others, influences those whom Christ calls us to serve, with whom we share the experience of His grace.

2. *"Go ye therefore."* Two words of the three have claimed a large share of attention among Christians. *Therefore,* referring to Christ's omnipotence, has pointed to an adequate though seldom understood or appreciated foundation for the directive. And the *go* has been translated into countless programs. But the *ye* or *you,* the pronoun of personal participation, somehow has escaped close attention. Or a distortion of its meaning has seemed to promote a limited directive.

The *you* supports and confirms the direct involvement of every follower of Christ in His mission. His mission of redemption becomes our mission. Our mission is truly *ours,* with no option, no reservations, no excuses. To have met Christ, to have received His forgiveness, to call Him Lord, involves us unavoidably in the reach of His love to men—our mission.

Unfortunately, the word "mission" has developed a very narrow meaning. In fact, a slight change to missions has robbed the word of much of its essential content. Missions has come to mean a program of preaching and help arranged for by a group of dedicated Christians. It has come to refer to a field of service somewhat different from the communities in which we live.

These meanings, generally accepted, have led to certain patterns of service. Other patterns have developed spontaneously in response to particular needs. In either case, much good has been accomplished. However, on the one hand, they have allowed evasion of the essence of mission. And, on the other hand, the patterns themselves have grown into "sacred cows."

Both situations are empty of meaning to a host of Christians who sincerely believe they fulfill "their mission" by supporting well-organized programs. All of this effectively hides the deeper Scriptural truth of personal obligation inherent in witness and mission.

The *mission field* had come to be known to many primarily as some country overseas. In recent years, almost self-consciously, Christians began to recognize that their Lord's commission could have an application on home shores as well. But in this context they have tended to limit mission to some remote rural area or to some depressed urban ward across the tracks. The Gospel is preached, too frequently with obvious condescension, to neglected and downtrodden segments of society. The redemptive work of Christ seems to have very peculiar geographical and social limits, whenever one analyzes our patterns of service.

This has made it possible for many Christians to detach themselves from direct engagement in mission. The simplest method of disengagement, as mentioned above, has been the faithful support of organizational efforts. The work of the church is considered to be compartmental. Christian education functions are carried out by one group of individuals. Elsewhere a committee is appointed to care for extension. Where the job seems too large, congregations band together and form a regional board.

For the still bigger job of work overseas, some regions join hands in a general or international organization.

Usually, considering the objectives, each of these developments has been based on valid premises. The rationale of shared responsibility is not to be ridiculed. Unfortunately, however, the logic of these actions is soon overshadowed by some of the secondary results. In the attempt to do an effective piece of work and sometimes meet a much more extensive responsibility, the church, meaning the members of the body, is almost completely bypassed. Of course, the roll call is taken at budget time or when the offering plate is passed. But the rest of the time real involvement in the mission of the church is carried on *in absentia* or by proxy. This is a flat contradiction of terms and a practical impossibility. This leaves the "you" out of Christ's commission to His followers.

Our system of service *in absentia* or by proxy has grown on us until many defend this as *the* way "to do mission work." The extension committee is responsible to organize a community survey or neighborhood visitation program. The regional board finds a city slum area at least one hundred miles away and ships in a platoon of Sunday-school teachers every seven days with dedicated regularity and singular shortsightedness. The overseas mission organization senses interest in a certain part of the world or searches out a nation with satisfactory visa arrangements and with areas not already overrun with similar expeditions (comity, you know), makes annual worker appointments, and organizes regular financial backing "to do together what we can't do singly."

As each of these three levels functions—local extension committee, regional board, or general board—the church is in business. Organization is effected, program is planned, funds are arranged for, workers are appointed, and activities are carried on. In general, this is a denominational pattern. And the picture is little different in independent movements, except for a less stable base or supporting constituency.

Let me repeat, the original concerns which called forth these developments have been valid. Thousands of dedicated Christians have given their lives through such patterns of service. And the Lord has blessed, many times in singular ways. But the enormous organizations spawned by legitimate concerns have almost totally obscured the true definition of mission. Consequently, the real field is consistently overlooked and a host of distorted impressions have been nurtured until the average Christian actually feels comfortable, even though he is utterly uninvolved in the mission inherent in his professed discipleship.

Our mission is to the world, certainly. Not to be neglected are the far reaches of this planet on which we live. But care must be exercised not to take an exception and make it the norm of mission. This we are prone to do when we point to the Apostle Paul's faithful overseas service to support our patterns. Thus we ignore the great number of unnamed Christians who gave daily witness of God's grace wherever they found themselves, in Jerusalem or "scattered abroad." These understood their mission; these had found their field, not in geographical terms, but in terms of persons who had not heard that Christ was risen from the dead.

"Go ye into all the world" includes every corner of the globe, without a doubt. This is precisely the point. Chances are, however, that a first reading of this sentence would be interpreted "far corners" of the globe. We have been so conditioned by patterns of missionary service in our generation that only a major conscious effort will include the "near corners" as well.

Even the use of a more specific term like "every creature" is no guarantee that the point has been made. For this term has been used so consistently in an overseas context that "heathen" pops up immediately as a synonym with attendant mental images that effectively screen the real meaning. We have been brainwashed into ignoring the relation of "every creature" to our neighborhood. Not likely has any of this been deliberate, but it has had the long-term effect of condoning a devastating vacuum in responsibility. And the format has hardened to the point where any question regarding the *status quo* is interpreted as disloyalty. Only a generation of faithful teaching can restore balance to the church's present emphasis and provide correct definitions for words like field, mission, and responsibility.

One other factor should be recognized. It was stated near the beginning and indeed lies close to the central thesis of this book. There have been earnest Christians who have understood their field in general domestic terms, as opposed to foreign. Zealously, they have pursued fellow North Americans to present claims of Christ. Unfortunately, however, their zeal too often outstripped wisdom and their efforts ended in failure. So they have welcomed again the comfortable delusion that witnessing should be left to the professionals—appointed workers under regular organizations.

But this is a task for all of us. You and I, who have been called to Christ, are commissioned by Him to reflect His life and love. This is *our* mission.

3. *"To every creature."* The question—to whom are we being sent?—has a simple, Scriptural answer. *To every creature.* The finality of the answer leaves no room for debate.

Our mission is to all men—to the human race. It is to persons. Persons for whom Christ died. Persons who have not known the grace of God, forgiveness of sins, new life in Christ, or reconciliation and restored fellowship.

Persons always form the audience for the message Christians proclaim. Not primarily depressed masses, hungry multitudes, new nations struggling for selfhood, or the neglected hordes inhabiting condemned tenements. Not masses, multitudes, nations, or hordes. Persons! Single individuals. Not faceless digits. But human beings with distinct personality traits and needs at once both universal and unique.

Fortunately, some of these people live near Christians. Unfortunately, many of these Christians have been so preoccupied with missionary maps, budget commitments, and prayer lists that they haven't noticed.

There is probably no Christian who doesn't have a mission field—*persons* to whom he can witness—at his doorstep. Unless, of course, he lives in unscriptural, antisocial isolation or has planted

himself in a segregated community open only to those who sub-
scribe to a similar brand of selfishness.

As noted earlier, the categorization of persons is a constant
temptation. Not only is this true in terms of categories of need
or response, but also in terms of interests. Businessmen's groups,
professional persons' groups, campus groups, nurses' groups, and
others are organized to get on with the job of witnessing. In some
cases, the person-to-person contact is encouraged but too often
with the high-pressure tactics alluded to earlier. Usually, however, when the evangelistic urge grips the group a meeting is
called; this, even though there seems to be something inherently
unnatural in a gathering organized specifically to reach non-
Christians.

But still the more serious element in this problem is the
splintering of audience. No one questions the normalcy of businessman witnessing to businessman or student to student. This
pattern can reap rich rewards. Indeed, its basic principle is synonymous with the thrust of this book's concern. Yet, to accept this
as a primary norm quickly tends to limit the perspective of the
Christian. He sees mission only in terms of categorical or group
objectives, not in terms of persons. Thus such a pattern tends to
perpetuate some of the distortions imposed otherwise upon mission and witness.

It cannot be said too loudly or too often that our mission as
Christians is to *persons,* regardless of background, race, profession, or wealth. Of course, the doctor is more likely to be a witness to other doctors than the farmer will be a witness to doctors.
And the insurance salesman will be a witness to others in similar
work as well as to clients. Obviously, however, every such person
will have a multitude of additional opportunities "to be the love
of God to people." And it is the shortsightedness of categorization which sometimes limits this witness.

Our witness obligation simply cannot be categorized—overseas, home; rural, city; professional, tradesman; housewife,
teacher. We witness not to masses or groups or categories—rather,
to persons. Geography is a secondary factor; we witness where

we are. The love of Christ reaches out, through us, to need. This must be the single conclusion as we "look on the fields . . . white already to harvest."

Nor can our witnessing be easily organized. If witness seems to require existensive organization, its essential nature is ignored. If it is limited to organized effort, the activities involved may not even be properly defined as witnessing. When witnessing is seen as a sharing of Christ's life *to every creature,* categories and organization drop away.

The person who needs Christ or a fuller understanding of the Christian way has, of course, certain needs which are basic and universal, inherent in his humanity; and other needs which are singular and unique, arising out of personal temperament, social background, external circumstances, and not infrequently from his own reactions to these factors. The combination makes him different, in some respects, from all his fellows, thus demanding personal relationships and involvement as a prerequisite to effective witnessing.

To every creature emphasizes a fine distinction in witness which must be noted. The thrust of the chapters so far has implied that witnessing is directed to the unsaved, to the non-Christian. In one sense, this should be true. It is Scriptural.

On the other hand, however, this too represents an unfortunate categorization. And it denies the real meaning of witness.

Witness does not need to identify the orientation of the hearer in order to shape what is said or done. Witness reflects the experience of a person. "That which we have seen and heard declare we unto you" (I John 1:3). The witness is given *to every creature.*

Actually, we simply reach out to share, person-to-person. In some cases this sharing will strengthen a fellow Christian. At times it may bring a twinge of conscience to the backslider. Or it may identify a hunger in the seeker and sometimes offer a long-awaited answer eagerly accepted.

Witness goes forth constantly from our lives. Under the blessing of God's Spirit, its message and reflection of grace searches out the needs in other hearts—Christian as well as non-Christian! This lifts witnessing to a level of maturity and impact which overshadows any other more limited view. And it represents most honestly both the secular and the Biblical definitions of the word.

A true witness of God's grace excludes no one. In reality, it is a nondirected or unfocused illustration of His miracle-working power. The Spirit provides the focus at the right time, in the right way, to one of the *every creatures*. This is His work.

4. *"Give ye them to eat"* was spoken to the disciples as Christ looked with compassion upon the multitudes, faint and hungry. The same directive comes to Christians today.

Hunger for food can be easily felt but seldom easily defined. "A pain down here" or "a gnawing emptiness" may be the closest one can get to definition of physical hunger.

The same is true of man's spiritual hungers. Definition is difficult. In fact, even the identification of these hungers as spiritual is difficult. Vague feelings of emptiness, anxieties, or feelings of guilt waft through one's spirit occasionally, sometimes settling down into a leaden burden. The absence of satisfaction or its temporariness grates against the consciousness.

A foggy apprehensiveness clamps the heart with fear, shutting off the small pleasures of life. Or a sense of separateness—from what isn't clear—floats through the conscious hours. Like a boat drifting, without a harbor, no other boats around—out of communication.

The word "hunger" seems to describe best the unverbalized longings many individuals feel, seldom can articulate, and never find answers for, even after frantic human searchings. Let us look at seven of the more basic and universal hungers which help to paint detail in the picture of the person to whom our witness is given. These hungers will be seen to have emotional or psychological overtones although they are essentially spiritual. Perhaps it would be more correct to say that spiritual food will satisfy the hunger.

a. The hunger for forgiveness. A sense of guilt, although

seldom called this, is always present wherever a standard has been breached. The standard itself may have no moral significance but a deviation brings with it an uneasy feeling, an expectation of reprisal, or at least a question regarding consequences. The only escape from this uneasy feeling is a complete personal anarchy and conscious decision to harden one's sensitivities to wrong. Even then one may question whether there are not still occasional twinges of guilt.

At any rate, the desire for relief from guilt is a hunger that grips the soul. From childhood and its list of prohibitions, the hunger has been present. Moral and ethical lessons in school and church and home have reinforced it. Where a spiritual standard has been raised, it will be the strongest.

The Christian Gospel answers this hunger through faith in Jesus Christ. Acknowledgment or confession of sin becomes the key to release from the bondage of guilt. For Christ has promised the forgiveness of sin.

b. The hunger for fellowship. Essentially man is a social creature. He craves involvement with and closeness to other human beings. He needs interaction with other people to complement his own singularity. Desire for utter aloneness, except temporarily, is abnormal.

However, sin in the human heart has undercut and destroyed the togetherness of the human race. Greed and envy have separated man from his fellows. Hatred and strife have set men in enemy camps. Petty grievances have cut off contact and sometimes destroyed the very channels of communication.

Instead of relationship, therefore, there is disunity. Instead of fellowship, there is enmity. Instead of togetherness, there is separateness.

The bread of Christ satisfies this hunger. Indeed, it satisfies the deeper hunger, often unrecognized, for fellowship with the Creator. The reconciliation which Christ brings answers this primary need. And miraculously, this restored fellowship with God makes possible a reconciliation between men as well—and fellowship.

c. The hunger for position. Although dressed in various guises, the desire for position, prestige, or status is never far from men. Partly, it represents a need for acceptance. More than this, however, this hunger reflects the nothingness men feel when cut off from a meaningful relationship with God.

Denial of this hunger ignores its universality. Recognition represents honesty and the first step to status through adoption into the family of God. Then follows the high call to be workers together with Him, ministers of reconciliation, ambassadors for Christ, kings, and priests.

d. The hunger for freedom. The hunger for freedom is also normal. The human spirit was not created to be bound. The individuality imparted to man confirms his innate right to be free. The power of choice and decision, given him by God, supports this right.

Slavery of any kind denies freedom and contradicts the will of God for man. He chafes under bondage—physical or spiritual.

Man's real problem, however, is not to admit his desire for freedom. It is rather to recognize the kind of freedom which is real and not an illusion. The breaking of rules, deviation from standards, rebellion, and anarchy do not actually constitute freedom. They only identify another master, whether it be another person, the physical senses, or the results any rebellious action will reap.

There is a bondage that leads to real freedom. That is an unreserved loyalty to Jesus Christ. "If the Son therefore shall make you free, ye shall be free indeed" (John 8:36). The Christian finds the freedom to be himself and in this a release of his real potential through the Spirit of God.

To this freedom the Christian gives witness.

e. The hunger for meaning. Meaninglessness characterizes many of our neighbors. When the gloss on material goods begins to dull and the senses no longer deliver what they promise, the heart hungers for some substantial meaning in life.

Intellectually and materially, there may have been precise objectives with fulfilled goals and a certain significance and meaning. Now these are seen to be inadequate and temporary and a new hunger grips the soul.

Meaning comes from purpose. And the only purpose which fulfills the essential character of man is that which God defined in creation. To be "in the image of God, after His likeness" brings man into tune with the universe and God's ultimate design. Of course, this new understanding colors all of life and satisfies the hunger.

f. The hunger for security. Actually this hunger reflects a deep need for love. To be loved, to be needed, to be wanted is a part of the nature of man. Unloved, he is insecure. Insecure, he is fearful. Fearful of present and future despair, not knowing which way to turn.

This hunger is closely tied to the hunger for fellowship. With people much of the time, he is still alone. In the multitudes he finds no mutuality. He bears his burdens alone. Intimacy tends to be physical and selfish. Lust and passion may be his bedfellows, but love eludes his grasp.

The absence of an anchor in love leaves him swinging at the mercy of the tides of casual contact. But here there is no security —because there is no love. And so the hunger gnaws away at his spirit. His silent screams for a home for his soul call forth only a selfish and temporary respite.

The Christian witness comes with a unique answer—Jesus Christ. In His love the hunger for security is met; without limitation, if His grace is fully understood.

g. The hunger for life. Much of man's frantic search centers in his hunger for a sense of aliveness. He wants to feel—vibrantly. He wants to know—certainly. He wants to do—significantly.

He wants to be alive. He wants to explore life. He wants to experience real living.

The sameness and detail of daily routine deaden him. The petty repetitions gall his sensitive nature. The emptiness of activity shrivels his spirit. The sour taste of spent passion nauseates him. His own selfishness boxes him in—into a tight little circle with no way out.

He wants to live! He wants to live largely, expansively, joyously. This need grows into a consuming hunger which never leaves him.

—Until he meets the Master who came "that they might have life, and that they might have it more abundantly" (John 10:10).

The task of the Christian witness is to introduce Him to his neighbors; to present the Bread of Life, the answer to his hungers.

This is *our* mission.

God sent His Son to save the world—

One night Nicodemus, a leading Jew and a Pharisee, came to see Jesus.

"Master," he began, "we realize that you are a teacher who has come from God. Obviously no one could show the signs that you show unless God were with him."

"Believe me," returned Jesus, "a man cannot even see the kingdom of God without being born again."

"And how can a man who's getting old possibly be born?" replied Nicodemus. "How can he go back into his mother's womb and be born a second time?"

"I assure you," said Jesus, "that unless a man is born from water and from spirit he cannot enter the kingdom of God. Flesh gives birth to flesh and spirit gives birth to spirit: you must not be surprised that I told you that all of you must be born again. The wind blows where it likes, you can hear the sound of it but you have no idea where it comes from and where it goes. Nor can you tell how a man is born by the wind of the Spirit."

"How on earth can things like this happen?" replied Nicodemus.

"So you are a teacher of Israel," said Jesus, "and you do not recognize such things? I assure you that we are talking about something we really know and we are witnessing to something we have actually observed, yet men like you will not accept our evidence. Yet if I have spoken to you about things which happen on this earth and you will not believe me, what chance is there

that you will believe me if I tell you about what happens in Heaven? No one has ever been up to Heaven except the Son of Man who came down from Heaven. The Son of Man must be lifted above the heads of men—as Moses lifted up that serpent in the desert—so that any man who believes in him may have eternal life. For God loved the world so much that he gave his only Son so that everyone who believes in him should not be lost, but should have eternal life. You must understand that God has not sent his Son into the world to pass sentence upon it, but to save it—through him. Any man who believes in him is not judged at all. It is the one who will not believe who stands already condemned, because he will not believe in the character of God's only Son. This is the judgment—that light has entered the world and men have preferred darkness to light because their deeds are evil. Anybody who does wrong hates the light and keeps away from it, for fear his deeds may be exposed. But anybody who is living by the truth will come to the light to make it plain that all he has done has been done through God." (John 3:1-21, Phillips)

7

THE RESOURCES

Resource is a misnomer when applied, without qualification, to witnessing. It can leave the impression of a storehouse to which we may go, optionally and spasmodically, if and when we need help. On the other hand, the word "resource" identifies or points to the Christian witness's absolute dependence on God as he lives his new life in Christ. Experience and resource are bound tightly together. To have enjoyed and to be enjoying this new life constitutes the only resource there is. And yet one cannot ignore both initiatory and supportive elements which make this experience a reality.

These we should like to look at briefly: the divine resources, the resources of personal experience, shared experience and shared knowledge, as well as the resource of modern communication skills and new awareness of the role they play in witnessing.

All of them have been stated or implied through the previous chapters. However, at this point, to lift them up and identify them as resources seems appropriate in order to emphasize their importance.

Before we develop these areas, however, let us look at a problem which often inhibits the recognition and use of the resources inherently available to the Christian. Unfortunately, these real resources can be hidden from view by assumed resources —patterns of Christian fellowship and service which in themselves may be valid but have deteriorated into negative influences.

1. *Assumed resources.* One may easily be misunderstood when referring to the church as an assumed resource. It can be a real resource, as we shall show in subsequent sections. But it sometimes also very subtly blocks the flow of redemptive power from God to man and instead of a help becomes a negative factor in the work of the kingdom.

This happens most easily when worldly patterns of structure and administration prevail. Most denominations and congregations are well organized. Organization is seen as a mobilization of resources to reach certain objectives. It can be. And to individuals who wish to share in the church's redemptive ministry, it should provide a resource and offer a channel for service.

However, the existence and maintenance of the organization can also become an end in itself. Programs are devised which, many times in their development, reflect spontaneous concern but in time grow into empty shells. Activities are engaged in which at one time represented Spirit-led effort but eventually degenerated into sterile exercises.

Few are honest enough to face the irrelevancies this can lead to. So the organization is perpetuated annually with its frantic activism hiding individual and corporate anemia. More than this the activistic perspective bustles past the real objectives of "church" and buries both the real resources and the desperate needs of men and women under an avalanche of utter irrelevancies.

Outreach directors and extension committees; missionary acres and quarter fund projects; tract distribution and jail services; evangelistic campaigns and regular worship services—all can be vitally significant or they can be nauseatingly irrelevant. So easily can they help the Christian avoid actual involvement with people. Instead of a resource and channel for service they blind the witness to the daily crushing misery of men and render him insensitive to Christ's example of coming "to seek and to save that which was lost."

Instead, then, of the organization or program or activity serving as resource through which need is met, they become devices for the evasion of personal responsibility.

For this pastors are sometimes to blame, and that doubly. In the first place, they have allowed the myth of lay noninvolvement to be perpetuated year after year. And secondly, they have allowed themselves to be constituted the major resource for witness and extension. The professional or ordained leader is seen as the prime moving force in both nurture and outreach. The laity shares in maintaining the pastor and in keeping organizational wheels turning. But this becomes the limit of their *participation*. In the Scriptural sense, this pattern can hardly be graced with the word.

Someone has said that the minister is necessary for the preparation of Christians to witness. However, for the actual work of the church in the world, he is largely unnecessary. This sounds harsh but may be closer to the truth than is generally thought. At least, Paul seems to say practically the same thing in his letter to the church at Ephesus:

"His gifts were made that Christians might be properly equipped for their service, that the whole body might be built up until the time comes when, in the unity of common faith and common knowledge of the Son of God, we arrive at real maturity —that measure of development which is meant by 'the fullness of Christ.'

"We are not meant to remain as children at the mercy of every chance wind of teaching and the jockeying of men who are expert in the crafty presentation of lies" (Ephesians 4:12-14, Phillips).

To consider much of the "regular" congregational programs as a direct outreach resource is to ignore the facts. Few "outsiders" will attend services if they can help it. Fewer still will respond warmly to any activity that seems to define them as objects of organizational concern. The congregation cannot say, "Here is the church; why don't you come sometime?" Only when there are the beginnings of personal involvement and relationship can rapport be developed.

This calls for both pastors and lay persons to move beyond their preoccupation with the extension of institutions and the "success" of programmed activities and to search carefully for the real meaning of the church in mission.

2. *Real resources.* The real resources are divine. A witness of God's grace can never be carried on without the recognition of dependence upon the supernatural. God's grace has made possible the miracle of a changed life. And His love flows through the ministrations of this changed life toward need. Nothing the Christian is or does, in a spiritual sense, can be seen apart from this fact.

Outstanding in terms of resource, is the continuing work of God's Spirit through individuals. Nowhere is this more essential than in daily living. This is the arena in which the continuing influence of a Christian testimony makes contact with people. Each human relationship opens the door to this influence. Unless the Spirit of God controls a life, only a negative or distorted witness will be given.

The Holy Spirit also leads in the direct and specific oral witness to Jesus Christ. If He does not, the result at best is a fleshly attempt at a spiritual ministry. At worst, it may destroy all hope for further witness because disgust at crudeness of approach has closed the door.

Actually, the Spirit works at two points. Through circumstances of many kinds He prepares a heart step by step. Then He seeks to direct, at the opportune moment, a witness of God's grace to the heart thus prepared. To run ahead of the Spirit can be as devastating as to refuse to follow.

The Holy Spirit, and His work in our lives as well as the lives of others, is a resource not to be ignored.

Another divine resource is the Word of God. However, the Scriptures are more than a cupboard full of proof texts to be selected categorically as tools to do a particular job on a given object. God's Word speaks to the Christian now. It reveals God's will. It identifies the Christian's pathway. And as he walks in this pathway, the direction of his life becomes the witness of God's love, of God's power for victory, and of hope made possible through Jesus Christ. His life is a testimony of peace and joy, of sustenance in the face of suffering, of confidence and trust even in the presence of uncertainties.

In the Word of God, the Christian finds his strength, his daily bread. As he meditates, he sees himself and his needs. As he partakes, he grows more like Christ. The Word becomes as necessary to his soul as food is to his body. The more he feeds on the Word, the greater impact his life will make on those who observe.

Having established this primary function of the Word as a resource for witness, one cannot ignore the direct and telling use of portions of the Word in the course of witnessing. This may be through written or published means or through oral expression. In either case, as the Holy Spirit leads, a powerful message can be shared with a seeking heart.

In the latter case, more is called for than a memorization of specified texts. This can be useful and should not be depreciated. But the Word of God fulfills its function as a resource when there is a personal and growing acquaintance with its riches. This goes far beyond the limits of an outline devised to answer certain categorical demands. Saturation of the mind and heart in the Scriptures is a prerequisite to the calling forth of those phrases or passages the Spirit of God may choose to use when speaking to someone.

The actual sharing of specific parts of the Scriptures, appropriately directed by the Holy Spirit, can speak to specific needs. However, without a doubt, the most powerful message is spoken whenever the Word of God is made flesh and dwells among men. The spoken Word can be ignored and contradicted. But there is no argument against the life which has been changed and is being changed. The Word and will of God "put into shoe leather" illustrates what is being said.

3. *Personal experience.* Apart from the divine resources, if

one can make such a distinction, personal experience is the fundamental resource available to the Christian witness. Without it, he will be limited to the exercise of some dead form, to a feeble preaching of moralistic code or a sanctimonious spouting of Scripture. However, with the personal experience of grace, a wellspring of sharing can be the result.

Since so much has already been said on this point, there is no need here for further expansion. It is mentioned only briefly to place it in correct perspective as the basic resource, the essence of witness. Without access to this, witnessing becomes a farce and the definition of the word completely distorted.

4. *Shared experience.* Perhaps next in importance to personal experience for the Christian witness is the mutual sharing of experience with other Christians. The witness to my brother and his witness to me is usually a prerequisite to the witness shared with a non-Christian. Unless this interaction between Christians becomes a normal and enjoyable experience, the witness to others will likely be somewhat stilted and abnormal.

Actually, as pointed out previously, the experience of witnessing, in its ultimate sense, is not selective of audience or context. Influence is not directed as at a target. The changed life is like a rose; its fragrance goes forth whether or not anyone is there to enjoy it. It is no respecter of persons. The fragrance is not lessened nor is it increased by the proximity of a certain kind of audience. The measure of fragrance is determined by only two factors —the character of the rose itself and the perceptiveness or sensitivities of the persons in its presence.

Having said this, however, one cannot deny that sharing deeply somehow seems easier in the presence of persons sympathetic to a viewpoint. The same should be true in the company of Christians. And yet, I am becoming convinced that one of the high barriers blocking the joy of sharing the Gospel with unbelievers is the singular silence between Christians.

For some reason, fluency of speech and openness is attained on practically any other subject—house furnishings, changing decor, exotic recipes, dieting, the stock market, the farmer's plight, a comparison of automobiles and their performance, the latest fashions, the best fishing, community affairs. This list could go on almost endlessly. Yet the mention of spiritual matters, for many, many Christians, is almost taboo. When the subject is broached, a haze of embarrassment often settles over the group. After a few worn clichés have been dropped into the awkward silence, someone shifts to the mundane and most breathe a sigh of relief.

Whatever the reasons may be for this condition, the condition itself is abnormal. As members of Christ's body, believers have much in common, in reality and potentially. Sharing with each other, unburdening one's heart, uncovering one's true self —this is a road to strength. But a reluctance prevails which literally denies the concept of brotherhood. As long as this reluctance persists, to speak of witnessing to the unsaved world is premature.

For the witness tells what he knows—about himself and God's work in his heart. The strength of witnessing is its honesty and forthrightness. Any covering up or distortion is not really witness. This kind of sharing must be experienced in the church, among believers, before it can be exercised elsewhere.

Of course, there is also a danger—that the comfortable sharing with others of like mind can blind us to sharing where the testing of our witness is faced immediately. The church is often charged with being an exclusive club; sometimes not without justification. A real peril of brotherhood is exclusivism—ignoring those outside. But this happens most easily where members of the "club" have only superficial ties. Whenever deep fellowship is enjoyed, and the Spirit is truly at work, there the movement will also be outward.

Not the least part of shared experience is the unity it entails. In fact, a major resource in witness is the relationship of Christians to each other. "Neither pray I for these alone, but for them also which shall believe on me through their word; that they all may be one; as thou, Father, art in me, and I in thee, that they also may be one in us: that the world may believe that thou hast sent me" (John 17:20, 21). This relationship of oneness makes a powerful impact on a society torn by pettiness and strife. Such unity can be kept and fostered only as members of the body become one in fact, as well as faith, through common allegiance to the Head, Jesus Christ, and mutuality with each other.

Shared experience draws Christians together. It stablizes convictions. It opens up new vistas of relationship. It prepares one for sharing more widely, outside the group of believers. It provides a retreat for restoration and new challenge.

Shared experience is of the essence of church. Members of the body can never escape their interdependence. And although each is called to a separate function, all join in reflecting the compassion of Christ in all of life.

5. *Shared knowledge.* Closely related to the personal experience of grace shared among Christians are those bits of knowledge acquired through various contacts with the unsaved. Only two are mentioned here briefly for what help they may be to those with less experience.

a. Leading a soul to Christ. As mentioned earlier, this step is sometimes considered to be synonymous with the experience of witnessing. But there is a difference. In the strictest sense, witnessing precedes the point at which a soul comes to Christ as the result of a specific personal decision. Witnessing involves the reporting of God's work in the heart, a simple testimony of His grace. When the time comes, and it may come only after long months of sharing, the witness may have the privilege of helping his friend relate to Jesus Christ in a personal way. Or he may be led of the Spirit to a stranger whose heart has been prepared by the witness of Christians elsewhere. In either case, some of the following suggestions may be helpful:

Show the need of men:

"As it is written, There is none righteous, no, not one" (Romans 3:10).

"For all have sinned, and come short of the glory of God" (Romans 3:23).

Show the judgment of God upon sin:

"Wherefore, as by one man sin entered into the world, and

death by sin; and so death passed upon all men, for that all have sinned" (Romans 5:12).

"For the wages of sin is death; but the gift of God is eternal life through Jesus Christ our Lord" (Romans 6:23).

Show the gift of God to sinners:

"For the wages of sin is death; but the gift of God is eternal life through Jesus Christ our Lord" (Romans 6:23).

"For by grace are ye saved through faith; and that not of yourselves: it is the gift of God: not of works, lest any man should boast" (Ephesians 2:8, 9).

Show that a personal decision is necessary:

"But as many as received him, to them gave he power to become the sons of God, even to them that believe on his name: which were born, not of blood, nor of the will of the flesh, nor of the will of man, but of God" (John 1:12, 13).

"That if thou shalt confess with thy mouth the Lord Jesus, and shalt believe in thine heart that God hath raised him from the dead, thou shalt be saved" (Romans 10:9, 10).

Show that one can be sure of salvation:

"For God so loved the world, that he gave his only begotten Son, that whosoever believeth in him should not perish, but have everlasting life" (John 3:16).

"He that hath the Son hath life; and he that hath not the Son of God hath not life. These things have I written unto you that believe on the name of the Son of God; that ye may know that ye have eternal life, and that ye may believe on the name of the Son of God" (I John 5:12, 13).

If the witness has been faithful and the Spirit of God has truly prepared the heart of the seeker, much of this will be only confirmation. Sometimes a brief review will be helpful. Other times the seeker will take the initiative himself and indicate a desire to become a follower of Christ.

At that point, the Christian may, almost casually, talk to God about his friend, thanking Him for the Spirit's work and the friend's decision. Then he can invite his friend to talk to God as well, suggesting that he tell God about himself, his needs, his sin, his desire to be forgiven; then thanking Him for acceptance into His family. It may be appropriate here to refer again to passages of Scripture showing the certainty of salvation. To many individuals, the step of faith, when it is finally taken, seems so simple they can hardly believe this constitutes a new birth.

b. Follow-up. The term "follow-up" reflects the technical approach to soul-winning. Many intricate formulas have been developed for follow-up work with new Christians. All have certain values, but some also have the disadvantage of complicating a basically simple concern.

The concern—that the new creature in Christ goes on in his relationship through growth to maturity. At the heart of this concern, two factors must be recognized. First of all, a work begun by the Spirit can be continued only by the Spirit. Galatians 3:1-3. No amount of fleshly effort can accomplish this objective any more than it can give a true witness of grace. Secondly, the requisites of friendship and involvement, so important in witnessing, are no less significant here. Another word to describe the experience is fellowship.

Actually, if the methodology of witness outlined earlier has been followed, there is no essential change in the relationship. The friendship ripens still further; the dialogue continues, only with added perspective; the involvement deepens, but now develops a dimension of mutuality. Of course, overlaying the relationship is a new joy in common understanding and a shared insight into and praise for grace. But the fundamental principles outlined for witness find a ready application even after the continuing faithful witness of God's grace has borne fruit unto salvation. In other words, relationship and witness simply continue.

6. Clarity. The first and final resource is a clear understanding of our responsibility as Christians and of the Scriptural definition of witnessing. So in further summary, let us note again a few of the major elements which characterize this approach and which can help witnessing to become an enjoyable, natural, and normal part of Christian experience.

a. Every person is a witness to something. In word and deed he reflects a basic allegiance, an aimlessness or purpose, a degree of satisfaction or meaninglessness. Every life exudes an influence. Every one is constantly reporting what kind of person he is or else he is kept busy holding one mask or the other in place—temporarily.

b. The Christian's witness consists of a report of his personal experience with Jesus Christ; the work of God's grace in his life; the changes which have now taken place.

He can tell of the difference in viewpoint, the transformation of personality, the miracle of birth into the family of God. He will show these changes as well—irritability replaced by patience, anxiety by trust, doubting by faith, self-indulgence by discipline, hardness by a tender spirit, an exacting perfectionism by gentle understanding, bitterness and resentment by love, discouragement by hope.

Naturally, these changes are a matter of growth. But to the degree they are not evident will the witness of grace be less complete. And the reflection of Christ's life will be distorted.

c. The witness simply reflects Jesus' life. He reveals the fact that he has become a partaker of His divine nature. He gives evidence of the Holy Spirit's control.

In this sense, to witness is not an obligation. It is a simple existential fact, the result of being in Christ. It is a state of being rather than doing. It is an announcement of the miracle of incarnation—the living Word, made flesh truly.

d. The witness is not called primarily to condemn evil. Jesus did not devote much energy to fighting evil. Rather, He showed constantly and consistently the goodness and purity of God. It was in the presence of goodness that men came to see their own imperfection.

Sin and need become quickly apparent in the presence of righteousness. The challenge in witness, again, is simply an honest reflection of the life of Christ.

e. Witnessing is a person-to-person experience. This does not ignore the validity of sharing with groups. But it does recognize the absolutely fundamental need for personal relationship to be at the center of an effective witness. This precludes mass anonymity. And it emphasizes involvement with the individual.

f. Involvement in need is the key to effective sharing. Until this takes place, irrelevance marks every attempt at sharing.

The content of witnessing implies its presentation in the arena of need. Isolation is antithetical to the character of grace.

Jesus came to the very frontier of human existence. He took upon Himself man's dilemma—his humanity. And He bore the implication of this humanity to the cross—inextricably involved to the point of supreme sacrifice. In this He accomplished redemption.

g. An irresistible magnetism exists between resource and need. Let resource be equal to Jesus Christ. Let need be equal to the results of sin in the lives of men. This divine magnetism brought Christ to men.

The same situation obtains today. Wherever the life of Jesus in His followers faces human need, it is drawn to it. The compassionate love of Christ flows outward. It gives itself. The true disciple of Christ cannot evade or escape involvement here. He stands, as it were, in the flow of that love, his every action controlled by it.

This is divine compulsion—the supreme motivation to witness.

h. Testimony can be both direct and indirect. A direct witness is focused specifically and, impelled by the Spirit of God, is a valid form. It can meet specific needs. This kind of witness is carried on more often in a transient context, although not necessarily so.

The indirect witness goes on all the time. It may be oral or nonvocal. The very nature of witnessing as an integral part of Christian living presupposes a great deal of this indirection.

Frequently also an indirect testimony makes the most telling impact. A bus driver pulled up to the bus depot in a small town for a lunch stop. Turning around, he said to his passengers: "The company doesn't allow me to advertise any eating places. But I just want you to know that if, in the twenty-five minutes we are here, you want for anything, I'll be across the street at Tony's first-class diner enjoying a nice, juicy steak and French fries."

i. Honest attempts at communication mark the Christian's witness—in deed and word. The deed will be a literal translation of the Gospel of Christ into understandable, concrete forms of action and behavior. The words will be simple and direct. They will be common in order to convey clearly the truth of God and the realities of personal experience.

The Christian will recognize that the average man is limited in spiritual understanding, not because of intellectual defects, but because of lack of exposure. He is truly an earthman, a man of this world, without the eternal dimension. Because of this, the witness must acquaint himself with terminology that will communicate to this earthman.

The familiar cliché will be interpreted or creative synonyms will be found. Each step in the sharing experience will prepare for new insights. Response will be sought. Dialogue will be encouraged. Since the ultimate objective is clarity and understanding, each concept and each word will be screened for maximum communication. For unless communication takes place, there is no witness. (See "The Witness's Dictionary," page 157.)

j. The Christian witness considers his calling to be honorable. Indeed, an ambassador of Christ holds a high responsibility. As a child of God he bears the name of Christ. The implications of this are not easily passed over.

He does not take the name of Christ in vain. Too often this idea is limited to the crude profanity of the street. Actually, the real profanity is to call upon oneself the name of Christ without following Him. To take His name in vain is to accept outward identification with Him and with His purposes, then to ignore Him and these purposes.

Unfortunately, this is the plight of multitudes today. Sincerely, or superficially, they have accepted Jesus Christ—they have taken His name upon themselves. They profess to be His followers, disciples indeed. But they remain in ignorance of their responsibilities of discipleship or lightheartedly they evade them. In either case, they have taken Christ's name in vain—to none effect, without fulfillment of the real purpose in his identification with Christ.

The true witness understands this. And he welcomes participation in Christ's ministry. Because he has experienced the grace of God he has something to say. And because Christ's Spirit dwells within he sees opportunities, again and again, to involve himself in the needs of men.

APPENDIX

The Witness's Dictionary

Part of the problem facing the Christian witness is his own private religious vocabulary. Many of the words in this vocabulary are found in the Bible. Others have been developed to define Scriptural truths. Most of them, however, are used normally only in Christian circles. Here they are understood, more or less. But when they are used among people who have had little or no religious background, the use of these terms without careful explanation or interpretation often leaves the hearer very much confused. Confusion begets the opposite of communication. Communication is the prime concern of the witness.

The following list of terms with explanations is offered, therefore, to illustrate the kind of interpretation which sometimes must be done. The Christian translates his language into the language of his friend, being certain to select words that have some familiarity and will carry the intended meaning. Obviously, this list is far from exhaustive. Rather, it is suggestive to show the kind of definitions which may carry more meaning than some of the more usual "Christian" words.

accept—to receive without reservation.

assurance—the state of being sure of God's friendship; absolute certainty of freedom from God's judgment of sin.

believe—to depend upon; to trust.

born again—the experience of change following faith in Jesus Christ. (The change is so radical that only this term describes it.)

brother—another Christian; implies closeness of relationship between Christians similar to that in human families.

confess—to admit openly.

condemnation—the declaration of guilt.

conversion—the experience of change in way of living which comes to the person confessing his belief in Christ.

damnation—God's judgment on sin.

devil—the fallen angel which is God's enemy; often called Satan or the evil one.

eternal—everlasting; for always; endless; when used with "life" refers to the quality of life God gives the believer in Jesus.

faith—the experience of complete trust in someone or something.

fellowship—deep friendship, having things in common with another.

forgiveness—God's act of *giving* His Son Jesus *for* us and forgetting our sin.

grace—the favor of God given to undeserving human beings.

Gospel—good news; usually refers to the fact of Christ's death and resurrection making possible for men and women a new kind of life.

heart—the real "you"; that part of you which loves and hates, chooses, thinks and acts.

heaven—the place of eternal fellowship with God.

hell—the place of torment and judgment; eternal separation from God.

lost—the state of being without answers regarding life; without direction and meaning.

reconciliation—the act and result of bringing enemies together into a friendly relationship; the term is used in the Bible to define the result of new fellowship between holy God and sinful man.

redemption—to buy back again; refers commonly to Jesus' act of sacrifice on the cross making possible man's return to God's spiritual family.

regenerated—the state of being re-created; to be made new again.

repent—to turn around and go the opposite direction in all of life.

righteous—the state of being right or just in God's sight.

saved—to be safe from the control of sin and the judgment of God.

Scriptures—the Bible; the inspired Word of God.

sin—a violation of God's law; disobedience.

soul—sometimes used interchangeably with "heart"; more correctly the part of man which lives on after physical death.

temptation—usually used to describe a test, a solicitation to do evil; sometimes a trying experience, a trial of faith.

unbeliever—one who refuses to trust Christ and receive the gift of eternal life.